VARIETIES OF FERVOUR

BRIAN LOUIS PEARCE

UNIVERSITY OF SALZBURG

Books by the same author include:

Poetry:
Selected Poems 1951-1973 (Outposts)
Gwen John Talking, (1985, Tallis; 1996, Stride)
Jack o'Lent (Stride)
Leaving the Corner: Selected Poems 1973-85 (Stride)
Coeli et Terra (Cornerstone, USA)
Thames Listener: poems 1949-89 (University of Salzburg)
"City Whiskers" in *The Playing of the Easter Music,*
with Caws and Caseley (Stride)
The Proper Fuss: homage to place, art and people
with autobiographical essay (University of Salzburg)

Fiction:
Victoria Hammersmith (Stride)
London Clay (Stride)
The Bust of Minerva (Oasis)
A Man in his Room (Stride)
Battersea Pete (Magwood)
The Servant of his Country (Magwood)

Plays:
The Eagle & the Swan (Mitre)
Shrine Rites (Envoi)

Critical/Editorial/Historical:
Palgrave: Selected Poems; edited (Brentham)
Thomas Twining, 1806-1895 (BOTLHS)
The Fashioned Reed: the poets of Twickenham (BOTLHS)
Essay on Ratcliffe in *Anthropos* by Eric Ratcliffe
(University of Salzburg)
The Palgraves to John Murray; letters, edited
(The Palgrave Society, forthcoming)

About the author:
Emotional Geology: the writings of Brian Louis Pearce
edited by Rupert M Loydell (A Stride Conversation Piece)

VARIETIES OF FERVOUR

PORTRAITS OF VICTORIAN AND EDWARDIAN POETS

BRIAN LOUIS PEARCE

UNIVERSITY OF SALZBURG
1996

First published in 1996 by Salzburg University in its series

SALZBURG STUDIES IN ENGLISH LITERATURE
POETIC DRAMA & POETIC THEORY

163

Editor: James Hogg

ISBN: 3-7052-0786-5

INSTITUT FUR ANGLISTIK UND AMERIKANISTIK
UNIVERSITAT SALZBURG
A-5020 SALZBURG
AUSTRIA

Distributed by:
DRAKE INTERNATIONAL SERVICES
Market House, Market Place
Deddington
Oxford OX15 0SF
UK
Tel/Fax: 01869-338240

CONTENTS

PREFACE

This book comes into existence because of certain lectures I have given at the National Portrait Gallery, London, on English poets of the nineteenth and twentieth centuries. The hope that they might be published has been expressed by those who appreciated them and the interest of Dr James Hogg and the University of Salzburg has made this possible. The book is devoted to Victorian and Edwardian poets, a coherent and well-defined category, who have much common ground, as well as their many distinctive qualities. The lectures were given to a lunchtime audience unfailingly benign. They have been re-written for publication and adapted to the overall concept of the book, and one or two pieces added. The book does not set out to be a comprehensive survey of Victorian and Edwardian poetry, however, given its original basis.

The length or scope of a study is not necessarily proportional to its subject. More may be taken for granted in the case of "colossi" who loom over a period, and have remained under discussion for generations; whose books remain in print and are on academic syllabuses, whilst those less in the public eye call for more exposition. Less quotation is required, too, of those poets whose work is on every library shelf and in many a private "bookery" as Walpole would term them.

The studies are both biographical and critical; primarily "portraits" from one intrigued by human individuality and creative psychology, aimed at inspiring interest in their subjects, but also embodying the responses of a practising poet with over forty years experience. This qualification aids empathy and exposition, it is hoped, and provides a basis for the author's views whilst not ensuring their freedom from idiosyncrasy (fortunately) or misconception. It is the writers' main thrust and individuality (or "inscape" as Hopkins might put it); what most makes their work itself, and what represents their "best" (or most active, intense and "successful") achievement that I have been at pains to search out. If readers turn again to the poets concerned, I shall have done my work.

It has been the particular hope of John Cooper (Chief Education Officer at the National Portrait Gallery) and myself that the lectures should recall to public interest certain poets who in recent years have not been given too much of a hearing. Which poets these are changes with fashion, and is a matter for the reader's own judgment, which it is hoped may shift a little as a result of this book. The Cambridge Bibliography of English Literature's practice of listing some authors as "major" and others as "minor" has always seemed to me a hostage to fortune. I have endeavoured to approach each poet with an open mind, and to appreciate that each writer's individuality may have value to certain (perhaps many) readers if only poet and reader can be introduced. That has been the purpose of John Cooper and myself, though neither would insist that it be called a vision. For the "Richmond Readings" which sought to light a smaller flame, amongst a similar discerning attendance, in the Old Town Hall, Richmond, Surrey, I alone can be blamed, as for any misadvertence in these pages. Those many persons to whom I am indebted, I acknowledge, with appreciation, at the end of the book.

Is there a concept or principle that holds these studies together?

Yes, the idea of "fervour" in all its variety, that intensity of feeling or belief without which there can be no creation, no outpouring of material that calls for the craftsman's control; that asks to be channelled and fashioned into the artefact. This question of "fervour" is the subject of the brief Introduction that follows.

There is one further aspect with which we are concerned here; that is with the persistence of Romanticism throughout our period and beyond it - for Yeats was by no means the last Romantic, as he claimed with the panache of middle age. The main part of the book begins therefore with a short chapter on The Romantic Inheritance, both as a general background to the poets and the period, and as an aid to tracing this particular aesthetic thread.

Brian Louis Pearce
Twickenham, May 1996

1. INTRODUCTION

Without fervour, some vibration or tension in the emotions, there can be no outpouring of creative material, to be given shape and form; no chaos to be ordered by virtue of the artificer's control. On the intensity of that "fervour" - whatever its origin - as, subsequently, on the art and control applied to it, will the "life-force" and validity of the artefact depend. The more intense the impetus, the sterner and tauter the control, the finer is the product that emerges from the mould: certain poems of Hopkins exert a claim to be considered as the supreme (or extreme) examples of this. This "fervour" or "excitement" can be of a general kind, such as many people will feel on a Spring day. It is always likely to have *something* of that in it; some related emotion such as grief, love, dismay, the feelings awakened by a person with whom we empathise or a particular piece of music. There is also another, more specific kind of fervour, that of a spiritual or philosophical character, involving conscience, commitment or restraint from commitment, conformity or nonconformity, belief or doubt, or a position of opposition. The two "fervours"cannot in fact be separated yet each has its relevance and importance, and in the period under review the religious question became of crucial importance for educated persons of conscience. There was the claim of the established Anglican Church; its exclusive control of university education, denied for so long to Nonconformists, Catholics and Jews - as, even longer, to women. There was the need for academics and clergy to adhere to the Thirty Nine Articles, and to conform in general if they were to retain Fellowships or livings. There was the need for public figures such as politicians to conform to the public image unless, like Disraeli, they possessed exceptional powers. The Anglican Church was itself divided by Tractarian and Evangelical tensions, whilst there were the conflicting but equal valid intellectual positions and appeals of Roman Catholicism (particularly appealing for someone like Newman who sought for authority); of Nonconformity, for those who sought and valued independency, freedom of conscience, and simplicity (who might speak of "the gathered church" or "the priesthood of all believers"); of doubters, like Clough; or atheists, like Swinburne; or what we can only call the "fervour of gloom" that we see in so much of Hardy, Housman and Gissing; of the aestheticism of Pater, Wilde and Yeats in varying degree, or of a "humane-ism" varying from that of Huxley to what in someone like Masefield[1] we might call a general, religious-based, well-meaning, kindly humanity, a condition that, from the Crimean War to the Falklands campaign, has been that of a good few. It explains the wrestling for faith or optimism of a Browning or a Tennyson, who were public figures, and the public roles they adopted. It explains the "High Romanticism" of Yeats, as of one born out of due time, pursuing those élitist poetic ideals of the free-thinking Shelley to which he, like Browning and Swinburne, was indebted. It explains the doubt and strain we find in Clough and Arnold and, in a milder form, in Palgrave. It explains the sincere response of Alice Meynell; the conviction by fiat of mind or will, as it were, of Patmore; the contention (and sublime mingling) of faith's ardour and the sensual man's fervour in Hopkins.

It does not matter, *from the aesthetic point of view*, whether the intensity or fervour be spiritual, sensuous, agnostic, aesthetic or scientific in origin; for the natural (given) world or for the things made by man, for the human or the Divine or the two combined; for man or woman, for the individual or the great body of mankind. What matters is that the energy, the fervour, should be there, and to a sufficient degree, save that where the "belief" aspect is present it may serve to give an added depth and pressure, an extra on-going relevance and, strangely, a keener individuality, to the writer who (so choosing) may seem to have thrown his individuality away. In the best poets and the best poems a high number of these attributes - spiritual and sensuous feeling, vision and control, personal response and universal relevance - all combine. Again, Hopkins is a touchstone, whilst Browning and Tennyson and, later, Yeats, often have greater range. The technical equipment of the poet is something that, in this introduction, we take as read. In what follows the presence of "fervour" will be implicit and questions will be asked of its intensity, its nature or variety, and the degree of control, in the case of each poet.

It remains to say this:

I. What a poet says or the poem he writes says may deceive us, not necessarily with ill intention. Wellspring or source "make" a poem what it is, but are not always explicit in the ostensible theme or subject. Take Arnold's "Forsaken Merman" or "Dover Beach".

II. It is not only the poets who differ in their intensity or their aims. We differ as writers and readers, and age differs from age. The legacy shifts, grows, declines, catches the light in different ways, as different readers respond to it, and re-assess what they find. It is shaped and known through the fervour of those minds in whom and by whom it continues to live.

Notes
1 He has a mystical streak, actually, while texts like The Coming of Christ and The Everlasting Mercy, put him firmly in the Christian frame.

2. THE ROMANTIC INHERITANCE

1. **"High" Romanticism** in England extends from about 1780 to the 1830's, so far as literature is concerned, though it is hard to put finite dates to a movement which has its roots in the Italian Renaissance, the English Renaissance (Chaucer, Spenser, Shakespeare and the Metaphysicals) and the European art, literature, music, and Revolution, of approximately the same 1780 - 1830 period. It persists through the Victorian years and into our own day. In certain obvious ways it can be seen to be losing its force - the Pre-Raphaelites lack the force of the High Romantic poets, and the Georgians lack the force of the Pre-Raphaelites - yet Yeats vibrates with it, and in many poets of the late 20th century, exposed to so many influences from so many countries and ages, it keeps the flame of idealism and aspiration alive.

2. **What *is* Romanticism?** One may offer first some phrases from the Shorter Oxford English Dictionary:
"The distinctive qualities or spirit of the Romantic school in art, literature and music."
"Romantic": lb Music: "Characterised by the subordination of form to theme, and by imagination and passion."
Of some Romantic music, but by no means all, it is of course true. In Keats' odes or Shelley's "West Wind" powerful emotion is controlled as powerfully.
2b: "Imagination purely ideal."
4b: R. movement: "the movement in literature (and art) originating in a revolt against the formalities and conventions of classicism, and characterised in the 19th century by conscious preoccupation with the subjective and imaginative aspects of nature and life."
We discard for our purpose those definitions regarding romantic fantasy or a tendency toward romance, which can be illustrated from the literature but are not central to the imaginative ideals of the movement. Every poet in his youth could be said to be a Romantic but that is a different answer and, strictly, too casual a one, though Wordsworth's and Arnold's careers lend support to the view.

Having set before the reader these sober definitions we will risk passing to the opposite extreme and set out some key concepts which will help to convey the spirit of the movement even if no single phrase necessarily applies to a particular poet or work.

Romantic literature is subjective, imaginative, idealistic, aspiring, aiming at self-realisation. It concerns freedom, expansion, and has links with political revolution, and may be said to represent the Dionysian element as opposed to the Apollonian. It involves warmth of feeling, puts "heart" before "mind" though in the best work both are combined and all due heed is given to form. It is concerned with love and beauty and the emotions; with the natural world, and the "sublime". The writers, and their characteristic heroes, may be seekers and pilgrims, questers who look for some actualisation of their imaginary visions and projections. (Self-) consciousness is exalted; an externalised quest may mirror an internal one, and passionate love and desire, whether for the Divine, the "Muse" a creature of clay, or for the creative act and achievement as an end in itself, works as an energising and "justifying"[1] force.

3. **The Cross-Cultural Connections.** Characteristic of Romanticism was Rousseau with his emphasis on Nature and on confessional exposure (of feeling) in literature as opposed to that of spiritual frailty in the privacy of the confessional, though it is true that St Augustine was a precursor in that. Writers like Schiller and (in part) Goethe played a part along with the music of Beethoven (the Eroica symphony), Schubert (Wanderer Fantasia), Schumann (the Manfred overture to Byron's play, or the Frauenliebe und Leben, Op 42, song cycle), Mendelssohn, Chopin, Berlioz. To these can be added the poetry of Foscolo and Leopardi, the painting of Delacroix, Turner and Blake, and aspects of the art of Constable.[2] In prose Carlyle was closely locked into the movement with his study of Frederick the Great; his interest in Schiller and Goethe, and his Heroes and Hero Worship lectures, one of which is on Rousseau, another on Napoleon.

4. **The Precursors.** English Romanticism reaches well back into the 18th century. Its agitations and exaltations can be traced in Gray's "The Progress of Poesy", Cowper's tragic "The Castaway", Christopher Smart's "The Song of David" - "Determined, Dared and Done" - the hymns of Charles Wesley, whose warmth of feeling is contained within such intelligence and judgment in lines like "Our God, contracted to a span/ Incomprehensibly made man" or his magnificent "Wrestling Jacob":

> Come, O Thou traveller unknown,
> Whom still I hold, but cannot see;
> My company before is gone,
> And I am left alone with Thee;
> With Thee all night I mean to stay,
> And wrestle till the break of day.
>
> Wrestling I will not let Thee go,
> Till I Thy name, Thy nature know.

It comes to early fruition in Blake, memorable for what he etched and painted as much as for what he wrote, an outstanding, original genius, author of lyrics such as "The Sick Rose", "The Tyger", "Morning", "Ah! Sun-Flower", or more extended pieces such as "Auguries of Innocence" or "The Everlasting Gospel", the latter a group of remarkable fragments from the Rossetti MS, the material purchased by Dante Gabriel Rossetti from Samuel Palmer; and the inspired seer of such prophetic books as *Milton, Jerusalem, Thel, Tiriel*, or *The Four Zoas*;

> Where dost thou dwell for it is thee I seek and but for thee
> I must have slept Eternally nor have felt the dew of Thy morning
> (Night the Ninth)

This brings us to:-

5. **High Romanticism.** The most intense period of English Romanticism comes in two phases. The first involves Coleridge and Wordsworth, who not only worked together on *Lyrical Ballads* but influenced each other. The imaginative afflatus of Coleridge as exemplified in "The Rhyme of the Ancient Mariner" or "Kubla Khan", the latter opium induced (or "bookery" induced, depending on how you look at it), is well known. Equally "Romantic" and beautiful work is to be found in his "Dejection" ode of April 4th 1802 which strangely mentions "joy" so often, and in his "conversation" poems such as "Frost at Midnight", "Fears in Solitude" or "The Nightingale", written at Nether Stowey. What could be more Romantic than "Dejection"?:

> O pure of heart! thou need'st not ask of me
> What this strong music in the soul may be!
> What, and wherein it doth exist,
> This light, this glory, this fair luminous mist,
> This beautiful and beauty making power.
> Joy, virtuous Lady! Joy that ne'er was given,
> Save to the pure, and in their purest hour,
> Life, and Life's effluence, cloud at once and shower,
> Joy, Lady is the spirit and the power,
> Which, wedding Nature to us, gives in dower
> A new Earth and new Heaven ....

- and in the next verse he speaks of his "shaping spirit of Imagination." It is a key Romantic poem, typical of that kind in which the "speaker" resolves (or seeks to resolve) some critical issue. Wordsworth's "Intimations of Immortality" ode, his "Lines written above Tintern Abbey", his "Resolution and Independence" poem, based on his meeting with the leech-gatherer, his expansive, high reaches, and sober record of fact, alike, in "The Prelude", his "Lucy" poems, his sonnets, all seem above such struggle, perhaps because he is near to Goethe in certain aspects, but, in fact, as in the case of Goethe, are not free from it. There is an undeniable width, depth and force in his best work, which however forbidding at times, draws admiration from us if through (very Wordsworthian) clenched teeth. The amount of his finest work outdistances most of his possible rivals. Of the second phase of Romanticism, Shelley seems most of his possible rivals. Of the second phase of Romanticism, Shelley seems to come nearest in scale, both by the amount of fine work produced in far fewer years, and by the high soaring wing of it, voyaging through empyreans unknown to most of his readers. He was an idealist, even if his ardour brought distress to some of those with whom he was intimate. Surely many of the highest peaks of Romanticism are to be found in the range that includes his "Adonais" elegy on Keats, "Prometheus Unbound", "The Cenci", "Julian and Maddalo", the "Ode to the West Wind", "The Triumph of Life" and the late lyrics to Jane Williams, a list which arbitrary and short as it is, illustrates the range and variety of his power and control. Keats' "Grecian" and "Nightingale" odes, his "Hyperions", "The Eve of St Agnes" and "Lamia" stand for a moment with them on the heights, though his (so ardent, high-souled) life was even shorter. Byron is too satiric to be quite at this level, though he is a man of ideas, and has his own "fervour", apart from the dynamism and lively reference of a work like "Don Juan". Plays such as "Manfred" or "Cain" had an angst and impact on the Continent which can still be felt today.

Amongst the names that could be added are those of Reginald Heber, who was to die in Calcutta, and John Clare, whose "Invitation to Eternity", Clock-a-Clay, "I am ....", and "I lost the love of heaven above" have the vital sap in them.[3]

6. **The Influences.** Keats "lived on" in Tennyson, Arnold, Palgrave, Alice Meynell, Hopkins and the Rossettis; in the sensuousness of Tennyson and the Pre-Raphaelites, and the ode-forms of Arnold and Palgrave. The "sensuousness" involved observation and feeling for detail, a descriptive (sometimes lulling) quality, and the attempt to "load every rift with ore." Shelley was a profound, vivifying influence for Browning, Swinburne and Yeats,[4] whether for his movement and sound, his intellectual idealism, feeling for freedom, symbolism, or sheer verve. Browning in turn influenced Hardy and Pound, and the "Keatsian" mode influenced Wilfred Owen. Masefield encountered these influences, along with the Arthurian, when he started in on English literature in New York. In Patmore there is a hint of Blake, and Blake was important for Yeats, too. It will be evident, however, that every poet is exposed to many influences and that observations such as these though well-meant as "clues" (and for the most part generally recognised) may be misleading at best.

There is one other type of connection, extra to that of one poet admiring, and being given impetus by, another's work. Patmore's father was a friend of Hazlitt and Lamb. Palgrave's father translated Foscolo, and was close to Byron's work, through his association with John Murray. Browning, an early devotee of Shelley, describes how he felt on encountering someone who had met him: "And did you once see Shelley plain?" In the tighter cultural circles such inter-connections were more arbitrary if no less important, than today. There was not the physical or social mobility of the 1990's, and persons of only slightly differing social status may not have met; yet there was neither the size of population nor what we might call "conceptual multiplicity", of today's world. Someone like Palgrave knew Tennyson, Clough, and Arnold; Patmore knew Hopkins and Alice Meynell, (as well as the Pre-Raphaelites), yet those two worlds will not have mixed much and there will have been some figures, like Housman, who stood, substantially, alone.

Notes
1 "for the once justified, I/ creak into our room" "Eye", *Thames Listener*, 167-8; the word is a familiar one in Paul's theology
2 See The Fair at East Bergholt, (1811), A Study of Sky and Trees, (c 1821), Hadleigh Castle, (1829) or other late, "dark" sketches done after his wife had died.
3 Based on lectures given at the National Portrait Gallery on Coleridge (19th May, 1993), Clare (28th April, 1993), Keats and Severn (9th September, 1992), and to plenary sessions at the Richmond upon Thames College.
4 "All the young of my time were his (Keats') disciples & Shelley's. They were, both, the undoubted poets. Wordsworth & Coleridge were marvellous men, no doubt, but to the young, both were grown up. K & S spoke to the young, & had disciples, Arnold, Wm Morris, Yeats." (John Masefield. *Letters to Reyna* (1983), Letter 390, 1962, page 339.
"... the sex, in an artist, is his impulse to life, to beauty, to all generosity & givings and forgivings. It seems to have run in Shakespeare like a sea, in Keats like a river of the South, & in Shelley like a moonlight cataract." Letter 202, 1958, page 201.
5 Then, as now, it depended if you were in them.

3. TENNYSON

Tennyson is one of the two colossi of our period, Browning the other. You may try to squeeze past them but you find you cannot; they are too large for you, and too much on the watch, despite having been around for so many years. Their names may have grown wearisome; their work may have been misrepresented, but once you read them for yourself you appreciate their scope, their sheer mastery; you realise how frequently you come across some extraordinary tenderness, some unexpected felicity of thought and expression, that sends a quiver of wonder through you like an electric charge. "Just when we're safest, there's a sunset touch", as Browning puts it in "Bishop Blougram's Apology". Though their more ambitious or better known work is not always their best, their range and scale exceeds that of any of their peers, except possibly Swinburne, until we come to Yeats, whilst, except for Hopkins, they excel all others in intensity, taking our reckoning by the dozen and not by the single poem. Amongst the many (admittedly generalised) ways in which we might try to sum Tennyson I have taken two (they differ only in emphasis) and will leave the reader to judge between them.

Diagnosis I:

In Tennyson it is the "darkness" that is the significant factor. It is a "darkness" born of his early life, yet in despite of this we find him struggling to find the light and to testify to it. The elements of "darkness" influenced his first forty years, crucially, so that it is a marvel that he "came through". They give force and definition to his deepest-felt, most characteristic poetry. To explain what they were, we have to go back to the roots.

Alfred Tennyson (1809-1892) was born at Somersby, Lincolnshire, on 6th August 1809. It is a very pleasant situation, on the edge of the Wolds, within walking distance of Horncastle,[1] but not too far from the somewhat desolate shores that lie to the east. The family was large. It was not well off. His father has been passed over in favour of a younger brother, so that there were constraints together with a sense of unjust deprivation. There was also a distinct "Tennysonian" melancholia, a brooding inability to face up to life, under the very roof of the Somersby rectory. The father would lie in bed until past noon. Of the seven sons, two turned to drink or drugs[2], and a third lost his reason. Tennyson called it his "black-blood" and always feared it, understandably. He was unhappy at Louth Grammar School, but was to go up to Trinity College, Cambridge, 1828-31. He conceived a passion for Rose Baring[3], of Harrington Hall, close to Somersby, but socially and financially she was far above him, and it cannot have eased his mind to compare his meagre resources with hers or those of his uncle's family. He was to be forty before he married and secured himself psychologically or gained artistic or national recognition. But the most crucial blow was the death of his Cambridge friend Arthur Hallam, to whom his sister Emily had been engaged. It is small wonder that he drank and smoked heavily even when famous; that his striving to be noble and elevated (as in "Idylls of the King") does not always convince today's reader, whereas a poem like "Tithonus" or "Oh! that 'twere possible" does, or that the anecdote of his saying that he'd jump off Richmond Bridge if he didn't "believe" suggests someone trying to convince himself. The remarkable thing is that he could affirm as much as he did, and produce such an outstanding public, patriotic-cum-faithful proclamation as the "Ode on the Death of the Duke of Wellington" one of the finest things he wrote.

Diagnosis II:

Only one thing matters in the life of Tennyson, poetically speaking, the death of Hallam. All his deepest, truest poetry is written relative to that. The few exceptions relate to similar crises.[4] The loss of Rose Baring gave rise to "Maud", which he never read or referred to without emotion. The "Wellington" ode itself is a response to an admired one's death, and Tennyson was a patriot to the core. It is true that so much of our poetry issues from some emotional crisis (be it Arnold writing "Thyrsis" on the death of Clough or Swinburne writing "The Triumph of Time" on being denied Mary Gordon, or Yeats' long-standing response to Maud Gonne), yet such is the *gravitas* of Tennyson's oeuvre and reputation that in his case the point can be overlooked.

Hallam (as much as the Knights of the Round Table or Prince Albert) inspired "Morte d'Arthur". Hallam inspired "Ulysses". Hallam inspired "Break, break, break". Hallam inspired "In the Valley of Cauteretz". Hallam inspired *In Memoriam*,[5] that sequence of some 130 poems written over some 17 years, to be finally published in 1850, giving him the financial security to marry Emily Sellwood, who he might have married as early as 1838 had he had sufficient income.[6] Had Hallam not died Tennyson would not have written *In Memoriam*. Had he not written it neither fame, marriage, nor the laureateship might have come his way; success, artistic and worldly, might have been denied him. So it is that his life leads up to, centres upon, and ultimately find itself in the death of Hallam. When Hallam died in Vienna in 1833, there were found these lines of his, that could serve as an epigraph for *In Memoriam*:

> I do but mock me with the questionings.
> Dark, dark, yea irrecoverably dark
> Is the soul's eye; yet how it strives and battles
> Through the impenetrable gloom to fix
> That master light, the secret truth of things,
> Which is the body of the Infinite God.[7]

That sums the Miltonic purpose of *In Memoriam*; to understand the dark things; to come to terms with them; to "justify the ways of God to men."[8] We may sympathise with Edward Fitzgerald's kindly meant comment that if "Tennyson had got on a horse and ridden twenty miles, instead of moaning over his pipe, he would have been cured of his sorrows in half the time", whilst finding such apt representation of how the heart *does* feel under such burdens; such delicate and felicitous interweaving of natural phenomena, such gradual lightening of the mood; so splendid a technical resource, variety of mood and lyrical flair, within the sober compass of these quatrains, such admiration for the thing's ambition and sheer honesty of fervour, that we might part with everything else he and six other poets had written to keep this. There is the hard won affirmation of the "Strong Son of God" prologue, part of which forms a well-known hymn, and of certain of the closing poems; the general brightening of tone and, least obtrusively, such things as the beautiful poem beginning "By night we lingered on the lawn":

Till now the doubtful dusk reveal'd
The knolls once more where, couch'd at ease,
The white kine glimmer'd, and the trees
Laid their dark arms about the field:

And suck'd from out the distant gloom
A breeze began to tremble o'er
The large leaves of the sycamore,
And fluctuate all the still perfume ...

The felicitous description of natural detail, and his ability to make "music" of sounds and their juxtapositions, his gift for phrasing, has often been noted. "Now fades the last long streak of snow" illustrates this with its alliteration, its use of vowels like "a" and "o" and its mellifluous "l" sounds. Some have thought him *too* mellifluous (not a fault of which too many of today's poets might be accused) and his Keatsian lushness of tone can sometimes be lulling. It is arguable that he might have benefited from Yeats' technique of preparing the fine line by others of a less intense or more colloquial nature (something Browning does well) rather than striving (like Keats, and in his words) to load "every rift with ore." As it is his splendours can wash over us. But not so easily ignored is the tender, sureness of touch of a line like: "Be near me when my light is low", while the lines "I seem to fail from out my blood/ And grow incorporate in thee" (in the poem on the yew) has a terse inevitability that prefigures certain things in Hardy or Housman, the accord between poet and environment and the way in which some universally understood but *personally-felt* emotion is expressed. The Danube to the Severn gave" should especially be noted, though it is its mood, not purely the striking mention of Severn and Wye in themselves, that seems to anticipate Housman. How personal to the poet's background is

17

the universally accessible:

> Oh yet we trust that somehow good
> Will be the final goal of ill,
> To pangs of nature, sins of will,
> Defects of doubt, and taints of blood...

If that poem's wrestle with hope does not quite convince, it may be that in its attempt to take a wide view it becomes too *im*personal for its own good, but what could be more sincerely expressive than the lines:

> So runs my dream: but what am I?
> An infant crying in the night:
> An infant crying for the light:
> And with no language but a cry."

He went to Twickenham; but couldn't stand it.[9, 10] It was too damp and low-lying and open to visitors. He moved to Farringford, in the Isle of Wight; found even that too accessible; ended up at Aldworth,[11] which he had built for him. "Maud" was published in 1855, the year when he was 46, and the first "Idylls of the King" in 1859, when he was fifty. By then his intensest, best work was done. There remained things like "Early Spring", a lyric commended by Betjeman, which shows spirit still willing, and skill still able, in an old frame, or "Merlin and the Gleam", deeper than it appears, with homage to Keats and Wordsworth, his early influences, implied in it. For a further dimension on the public figure, see the letters exchanged between him and the Queen in Hallam Tennyson's memoir. One may think them sycophantic, and be glad to have escaped such a performance, or feel that they show a man of great simplicity and honesty, a deep, true nature, and that the "dark" but genuine interior redeems the gruff reserve-cum-vigour of the enclosing persona, and that the letters (if inevitably too much about grief) do credit to both writers.[12, 13, 14]

Notes:
1 A statement the writer has tested on foot. The environs of Bag Enderby and Harrington Hall may be compassed within the same day's peregrination.
2 But it led to no "Kubla Khan" though so many of the sons wrote verse.
3 Of the banking family whose name is still before the public.
4 One senses that the fine but claustrophobic "Mariana" poems and "The Lady of Shalott" which have the flavour anticipatory of some Pre-Raphaelite work, stem chiefly from intense feeling transferred empathetically to the women.
5 That sequence so unfortunately, gloomily, titled.
6 The engagement was broken off in 1840, her father being uneasy at Tennyson's morbidity and lack of means.
7 Lines by Arthur Hallam cited in *Tennyson: a memoir*, by his son (Hallam Tennyson), 1897 (1906), 88; (the book includes memoirs by Jowett, Palgrave, and others).
8 *Paradise Lost*, Bk.I, line 26
9 For the Twickenham period see Pearce, B L *The Fashioned Reed*, 1992, 33-37
10 The author had the pleasure of working with the late Gemma Hunter on the Orleans Gallery Tennyson exhibition of 1992 and would like to pay tribute to her creativity and

kindness.
11 Near Haslemere.
12 See Ref. 7, 782-800
13 Subject of a "Richmond Reading" of 29.10.1992.
14 Charles Tennyson's *Alfred Tennyson*, 1949, should also be consulted.

4. BROWNING

Robert Browning (1812-1889) was the closest to Nonconformity of the poets discussed in these lectures, if we may discount Patmore's marriage to a Congregational minister's daughter. His mother was of a Calvinist Presbyterian tradition[1] and during his formative years Robert attended the York Street Independent chapel in Camberwell. It is true that the picture he draws in "Christmas Eve and Easter Day" or the Bunyan-esque "Ned Bratts" for that matter, is not all that sympathetic. Yet his lifelong moral concern; his sense of the need for personal response to the demands of "justice" and the countervailing possibilities of "mercy"; his confessional "feel"; his approval of persons standing on their own; his preoccupation with self-realisation; his zeal for both righteousness and achievement; his sense of a spiritual dimension; above all what can aptly be termed his moral generosity, testifies not only to certain values that he shared with his time, but to the long-lasting alliance of Dissent with Shelley in the formation of his ideas, though with the more innate (rather than the most vocal or chronicled, it may be) of Dissent's governing ideas. For Dissent is not only about "sobriety, frugality, measure", the kind of concept on which Browning was reared, but about tension, energy, *contrappusto*, if Daniel Jenkins is to be believed,[2] which need not mean hysteria or ill-taste. The influence of Shelley came hard on the heels of that of Independency. It produced "Pauline" and "Sordello" as well as strengthening his interest in Italy. The outcome seems to suggest that, despite Shelley's free-thinking, his influence is not much at odds with Nonconformity in relation to poetic activity. The fervour of each is remarkably similar, and the author of "Adonais", "Prometheus Unbound", and "Julian and Maddalo" no unworthy hero for his young, morally-reared disciple. That Browning's mother persuaded her son to return to the fold in despite of Shelley's influence was not crucial ultimately - by the autumn of 1828 he had ceased to attend the York Street chapel "on any regular basis"[3] - though he felt his own submission as a failure of conscience and it may have retarded him temporarily. His acquaintance with Lizzie and Sarah Flower (the latter the author of "Nearer, my God to Thee"), and Lizzie's relations with the Unitarian W J Fox will have broadened the future author of *Men and Women*'s[4] mind and provided emotional impetus.[5] So we find two forces that contend within him or, rather, combine to advantage: the concern with a man or woman's "*soul*" and the concern with their fulfilment and "freedom", their truest "*happiness*". The Romantic and Dissenting strands are difficult to unravel there, and their coming together in Browning's broad, generous mind fuses an achievement that rivals Tennyson's in outliving its age.[6,7] Though like Tennyson he tends to be bracingly optimistic and edifying, he continually demonstrates compassion and a deep understanding of the frailties and aspirational ambiguities of humanity. He sympathises with his characters, and often likes them, one feels, much as he may show them giving themselves away as they speak. He is not them but speaks through them. A good many of his heroes are semi-achievers, would-be aspirants; trying to take wing, but finding their feet dragging on the ground. To that extent, he himself does better than them. His psychology and power of description are of a high order, and he (like Yeats) is particularly good at the way he takes us into a poem, using colloquial reference or jargon, as Hardy and later writers were to do after him. In certain surprising ways this is not so dissimilar from Hopkins' method, who shares his moral and religious concern, but Browning, in his dramatic monodramas, is unique in the way he plunges us into a poem or situation. In 1846 he married the "invalid" Elizabeth Barrett (herself a poet whose work was read) and moved to Italy, where he lived till (in 1861) she died. This residence, together with his wide reading and deep interest in the arts, helped to give an extra width, an "extra-English" dimension, to a cultured nature already sufficiently intense. His is a cerebral as much as an emotional fervour. His best work dates from his early maturity and his mid-career, principally from his Italian and married years though not necessarily or exclusively so. His later work is apt to be devilled with didacticism (always his trap) and titles designed seemingly to deter the reader from venturing nearer by their bumbling esoteric deflation. Yet his lyric touch can be as true as ever; the gleams of personal truth glimmer (like Tennyson's "Gleam") to the end as in "Never the time and the place" or the touching small things such as "Dubiety", "Humility", "Now", "Summum Bonum","Inapprehensiveness", or the fine Prologue, in *Asolando*, his last book. He might have written fiction. As it is he gives us a "picture gallery" of immense range and vitality in his verse: psychological dramas, self-revelations (ostensibly of his characters), lyrics, narratives, scraps of personal memories and affections, the peaks that rise through *The Ring and the Book*. His readability and colloquial tone ensures readers; his lyric gift touches them and holds them; his apparently artless and conversational style, its confiding and discursive manner, influenced Ezra Pound amongst others. His achievements may be summarised as threefold:

1. *The Ring and the Book*, in its twelve "books". Amongst its best things is the Pompilia book, though the different angles and viewpoints of "Half Rome" may be the more readable (and wry) way in to the series. The Pope's striking image of the sky at Naples, daunting as it may be in its application as he sees it, is what most remains with this reader;

2. *The psychological monodramas*. The best of these are in *Men and Women* (1855) equal as a volume to "*In Memoriam*" or Keats's *Lamia* ... though so

different; full of insight and invention, range and original power, with such variety in subject, style, length, mood. It ranges from the sensuous worldliness of "Fra Lippo Lippi":

> Flower o' the broom,
> Take away love, and our earth is a tomb

to the asceticism of "A Grammarian's Funeral":

> Here's the top peak! the multitude below
> Live, for they can there.
> This man decided not to Live but Know –
> Bury this man there?

– from lyrics to the massive soul-scape of "Bishop Blougram's Apology" – to the varying moods, chuckles, theology, humanity of which one extract scarce does justice:

> Just when we're safest, there's a sunset-touch,
> A fancy from a flower-bell, some one's death,
> A chorus-ending from Euripides, -
> And that's enough for fifty hopes and fears
> As old and new at once as Nature's self,
> To rap and knock and enter in our soul ...

– from the fine shades of compromise as delineated in "Andrea del Sarto" to the emotion and conviction of "Saul":

> I know not too well how I found my way home in the night.
> There were witnesses, cohorts about me ...
> Angels, powers ...

– from the missed opportunity which the poet regrets in "The Statue and the Bust":

> I did no more while my heart was warm,
> Than does that image, my pale -faced friend.

– to the quest accepted in "Childe Roland to the Dark Tower Came", where Shakespeare and Bunyan contribute to a rich text that prefigures MacNeice's play *"The Dark Tower"*, if not Eliot's "Waste Land" of equally personal origin:

> Fool, to be dozing at the very nonce,
> After a life spent training for the sight!
> ...
> Names in my ears,
> Of all the lost adventurers my peers, -
> How such a one was strong, and such was bold.
> And such was fortunate, yet each of old
> Lost ...

– from the austere Shelleyian vision of the poet as "unacknowledged legislator" in "How it strikes a Contemporary":

> Doing the King's work all the dim day long,
> In his old coat ...

– to the warmth of "One Word More" (to E.B.B):

> God be thanked, the meanest of his creatures
> Boasts two soul-sides, one to face the world with,
> One to show a woman when he loves her.

Before *Men and Women* came "Waring", "The Flight of the Duchesss", "The Bishop Orders his Tomb at St Praxted's Church" and such anthology pieces as "Home thoughts from abroad", "My Last Duchess", "Porphyria's Lover", "The Pied Piper of Hamelin" and "How they brought the Good News from Ghent to Aix", in which there is already so much variety of psychological insight and energy of utterance. After it there would come "Abt Vogler", "Rabbi Ben Ezra", "A Death in the Desert", "Caliban upon Setebos", and "Mr Sludge 'The Medium'", riches enough - not to speak of *The Ring and the Book*;

3. *The lyrics* and personal poems of such marvellous zephyr and inevitability in which he "hits the target" time after time. Few poets of his period come near to him in this, Tennyson, Hardy and Yeats, each at times. It is an aspect of his work that can be overlooked, yet in this, as in his psychological metier, he excels.

"Meeting at Night" or the song "Nay but you" show his earlier capacity. In *Men and Women* there is "A Woman's Last Word" with the sure simplicity that few but he and Hardy can manage, or the wizardry of "Two in the Campagna", one of the dozen most masterly Victorian lyrics, arguably:

> The champaign with its endless fleece
> Of feathery grasses everywhere!
> Silence and passion, joy and peace,
> An everlasting wash of air -
> Rome's ghost since her decease.
>
> Such life there, through such length of hours,
> Such miracles performed in play,
> Such primal naked forms of flowers,
> Such letting Nature have her way
> While Heaven looks from its towers.
>
> How say you? Let us, O my dove,
> Let us be unashamed of soul,
> As earth lies bare to heaven above.
> How is it under our control
> To love or not to love?
>
> ...
>
> No. I yearn upward - touch you close,
> Then stand away. I kiss your cheek,
> Catch your soul's warmth, - I pluck the rose

And love it more than tongue can speak -
Then the good minute goes.

Already how am I so far
Out of that minute? Must I go
Still like the thistle-ball, no bar,
Onward, whenever light winds blow,
Fixed by no friendly star?

Just when I seemed about to learn!
Where is the thread now? Off again!
The old trick! Only I discern -
Infinite passion and the pain
Of finite hearts that yearn.

– a touchstone for the lyric, as Hardy and Yeats will have known. In the lighter
"Women and Roses" there is anticipation of Yeats, in fact. In *Dramatis
Personae* (1864) there is "Confessions" (very Hardy-esque in its setting)
ending:

How sad and bad and mad it was -
But then, how it was sweet!"

– "May and Death" on the loss of his early friend James Silverthorne,[8] showing
such delicacy of feeling and phrasing; "Prospice", "Youth and Art" (a "poor
man's" "The Statue and the Bust", perhaps), and "A Face", a marvellously
persuasive response to Patmore's first wife (who was also painted by Millais),
which appears so "offhand", so "dashed down" and yet because of that, which
is its very art, still glows on the page today:

If one could have that little head of hers
Painted upon a background of pale gold,
Such as the Tuscan's early art prefers! ...

One wonders what Patmore made of it. Was he jealous or proud?[9]

Late in his life, when other poets would publish only what passed for
edifying, he gave us "A Tale", a marvellous compliment to the woman he had
in mind and to the gender in general; "Fears and Scruples", so telling a spiritual
allegory of loyalty and doubt that it is a pity he has to "dot the i" at the end; those
last poems in *Asolando*, published in his late seventies in the week of his death,
and the simple truth of "Never the time and place/ And the loved one all
together!" which everyone must have felt but no one else had expressed.

For other reactions to Browning's achievement see ref. 7 below, or that of
F T Palgrave[10, 11, 12]

Notes
1 With Scottish and Dutch strands, cf. Mairi Calcraft's immensely informative study: "Robert
Browning's London: 1812-1889." Browning Society Notes, 19 (1989), 1-134, with illus &
maps (esp. 8, 19-22, 25-26, 30 etc in this context)

2 Daniel Jenkins: "A Protestant Aesthetic?" *Journal URC Hist Soc. 3* (9), Oct 1986, 368-376 (Bunyan and Charles Wesley speak for him)

3 Ref 1, 31

4 An outstanding book, equal to Keats' *Lamia* ... (1820) in richness.

5 Donald Davie: *A Gathered Church*, 1978, brings out the varied strands of Nonconformity, and the cultured, intellectual calibre of Unitarian or Congregational families such as the Martineaus or the Gaskells (and at a more modest level that of William Hale White, "Mark Rutherford"); Browning's home background was of this kind (cf. the 6,000 books in his father's library) whatever the varieties of fervour he experienced week by week in the worship of the chapels around him. See also Davie's *Dissentient Voice*, 1982, 32-47 (38, eg.)

6 Though his work was somewhat in eclipse at certain periods earlier in the twentieth century, appreciation has both continued and revived, so that we find the *Oxford Anthology of English Literature*, Vol. 2, 1973, (1279) prepared to put his name first amongst Victorian poets.

7 Amongst many editions and selections to be commended are:- *Browning: poetry and prose*; selected by Simon Nowell-Smith. Rupert Hart-Davis, 1950, and (more by way of an introduction) *A Centenary Selection from Robert Browning's Poetry*; edited by Michael Meredith. Browning Institute/Constable, 1989. See also the Oxford English Texts, or *The Poetical Works*, Smith Elder & Co, 1898 (eg.)

8 Neal, J: "The Silverstone Family". *Browning Society Notes, 21*, 1991-2, 61-65

9 By the time of *Dramatis Personae*'s publication, as it happens, sadly the lady had died.

10 Pearce, B L: "Browning and F T Palgrave: some notes". *Browning Society Notes, 21*, 1991-2, 65-69; see also Appendix I below.

11 Subject of a "Richmond Reading" of 21st February 1991.

12. The Independent chapel off Church Lane, Ledbury (now the Burgage hall) was an early example of ecumenism in Old Dissent, being both Congregational and Presbyterian. Elizabeth Barrett's attendance, if proven, makes an interesting parallel with Robert Browning's early background.

5. THE BALLIOL SCHOLARS

"The Balliol Scholars", of whom J C Shairp writes so movingly, included Shairp himself (1819-85), Principal of United College, St Andrews, and Oxford Professor of Poetry 1877-1885; Clough, Arnold and Palgrave, each of whom is given separate treatment below, and Frederick Temple, the future Archbishop of Canterbury. Arnold (in 1857-67) and Palgrave (in 1885-95) were Professors of Poetry too.[1] Palgrave, like Patmore, has been too long out of print.[2] He has an historical sense; some of his hymns are still used, and there are lyrics that still speak to the reader. Clough was particularly important to the group. In "A Remembrance" Shairp writes:

Foremost one stood with forehead high and broad ...
All travail pangs of thought too soon he knew,
All currents felt, that shake these anxious years,
Striving to walk to tender conscience true,
And bear his load alone, nor vex his peers ...
(Clough)

The one, wide-welcomed for a father's fame ...
We see the banter sparkle in his prose,
But knew not then the undertone that flows
So calmly sad, through all his stately lay ...
(Arnold)[3]

Shairp wrote hymns, as well as the Highland evocations that Palgrave assembled in Glen Desseray, (1888) edited as a pious labour after Shairp's death. But his most touching legacy is "The Bush aboon Traquair" with its "auld scrunts o'birk" which had once flourished in beauty and been host to many a tryst:

...
And what saw ye there,
At the bush aboon Traquair? ...

They were blest beyond compare
When they held their trysting there,
Amang thae greenest hills shone on by the sun;
And then they wan a rest,
The lonest and the best,
I' Traquair Kirkyard when a' was done.

Now the birds to dust may rot,
Names o' luvers be forgot ...
But the blyth lilt o' yon air
Keeps the bush aboon Traquair,
And the love that ance was there, aye fresh and green.[4]

The mood of "A Remembrance" chimes with that of Arnold in his Thyrsis elegy for Clough, and evokes the same nostalgia for brotherhood, talent, and early hopes and ideals now fled. It was Clough who was the bright hope; the one they all remember; the one, indeed, who got away, and not only by going to America; whose failure to achieve what was expected of him (a little like Coleridge's) was evident before his too early death. Yet the play of his thoughts and something deeply sympathetic in his idealism, stays with us as an essence in our minds (again as in the case of Coleridge). Arnold has to be considered the most resonant and influential writer, taking into account his poetry and his critical work, but Clough's original and sensitive intelligence, his irony and vitality, his doubt, link him very much to our own day.[5]

Notes

1 As was Palgrave's relative Francis Hastings Doyle, 1810-88 (Professor 1867-77) author of "The Private of the Buffs" in *The Return of the Guards*, 1866 - published principally with the Professorship in view (cf. the preface) - and no Balliol man.

2 But see the *Selected Poems*, Brentham Press, 1985; edited by the present writer.

3 Quoted in Pearce, B L *The Fashioned Reed,* BOTHLS, 1992, 31-33

4 The full text of "A Remembrance" and "The Bush aboon Traquair" can be found in Grant Duff's *Victorian Anthology*, Sonnenschein, 1902, 229-238.

5 Based on a talk given at St Albans to the Ver Poets, 4.2.91

6. CLOUGH

Arthur Hugh Clough was born at 9 Rodney Street, Liverpool, on 1st January, 1819. His grandfather was a wealthy Canon who lost his investments when a bank failed. His father, James Butler Clough, sought his fortune in Liverpool as a cotton merchant, marrying Anne Perfect, daughter of a banker from Pontefract. There were four children, Arthur being the second and Anne Jemima Clough (1820-1892), the first principal of Newnham College, the third. When Arthur was four, his father decided to try his fortune on the American side of the Atlantic cotton trade, at Charleston, South Carolina. Here the family remained rather "English" and exclusive. Arthur was taught at home and was thus in for a rude awakening when brusquely separated from his mother and transported back across the Atlantic to a boy's school in Chester. In 1829, at the age of nine, he proceeded to Rugby, where the redoubtable Dr Thomas Arnold (father of the poet) had only recently become headmaster, at the early age of thirty-three. Arnold was set upon a religious, moral and intellectual reformation in education. What he looked for was "1st, religious and moral principles; 2nd, gentlemanly conduct; 3rd, intellectual ability. His lance was set against the irregularity and irreligion to be found in his day. What he did not change was the fagging and prefectorial system which he inherited, or the use of corporal punishment for offences real or perceived and, though known to have apologised in front of the whole school when he had picked on the wrong boy, there remains a severity about the regime, and a claustrophobic moral concern, despite the ideals in view and the undoubted sincerity and fine qualities of the Doctor to whom his son was to pay deserved and moving tribute in "Rugby Chapel". It was into this atmosphere that Clough came. Mrs Arnold showed him kindness, recognising his sensitivity. He had his friends, and seems to have coped well with his studies. But too early a responsibility was placed on him in his last years at Rugby which, in conjunction with his mother's absence in America, may have done him serious injury. A spirit of fecund liveliness, potentially, was crammed into a mould of premature seriousness, as gradually he became a pupil on whom (Thomas) Arnold set his highest hopes. He was earnest, industrious, and highly endowed. He won prizes. He played football with spirit. In the sixth form he became increasingly Arnold's willing disciple; his efforts and personality being commandeered in the service of the headmaster's ideals. Chorley[1] writes: "It is said that seated on the Doctor's right in the library he would look up into his face with an almost feminine expression of trust and affection in answering his questions or hanging on his words." In 1837 he went up to Balliol College, Oxford, to which he had won a scholarship. There he met Shairp, F T Palgrave, Frederick Temple, the future Archbishop, and consolidated his friendship with Tom and Matthew Arnold,

Dr Arnold's sons. It was Tom with whom he was on the most intimate terms, but Matthew who was to write "Thyrsis" in his memory. From an early date he was almost over conscientious and sensitive on religious issues, and there is no doubt that this scrupulosity took toll of his psychological resources. It may have been partly responsible for his failure to obtain the First Class degree that everyone expected.[2] In 1842 he put the record straight by gaining a Fellowship at Oriel. Difficulties in subscribing to the Thirty Nine Articles harassed him, however, and in 1848, when approaching thirty, he resigned his Fellowship. The step was decisive; strong-minded, but disastrous, seen with hindsight, for never again was he to find a milieu so comparatively well suited to his temperament. He was of a scholarly nature, and was intellectually adequate to the tasks demanded of him. He had friends, and tutees, and the reading parties that would fructify in "The Bothie ...", his first major poem. Resigning his fellowship worsened a financial position already constrained by a downturn in his father's business. Dr Arnold, who represented a point of stability, died in 1842; his father and brother George died soon afterwards. It is doubtful if he foresaw all the consequences of his resignation. Apart from his peers - in particular the "Balliol Scholars" - he was on his own. On his own, seeking vainly, as he puts it:

one feeling based on truth

He finds himself, in another fragment of circa 1840:

Like a child
In some strange garden left awhile alone ...
Plucking light hopes and joys from every stem,
With qualms of grave misgiving in my heart
That payment at last will be required,
Payment I cannot make, or guilt incurred,
And shame to be endured.

A more amusing, equally characteristic, presentation of his feelings at this time can be found in the poem "Duty":

Duty - that's to say complying
With whate'er's expected here;
On your unknown cousin's dying
Straight be ready with a tear ...

T'is the stem and prompt suppressing,
As an obvious deadly sin,
All the questing and the guessing
Of the soul's own soul within.

Perhaps his mood is summed up on this line from "Amours de Voyage":

Action will furnish belief but will that belief be a true one?

There it was: his integrity, his spirit of enquiry, his enthusiasm, his concern for truth and ideas, his preoccupation with duty, that stood him in good stead as a tutor and, with his playful irony of spirit, charmed his friends. His Balliol Scholar peers, warmed by that charm, impressed by his high-mindedness and outstanding mental powers, could only lament that the accompanying perception of ambiguity, and his anxiety concerning it, thwarted those powers and prevented them fructifying readily in artefact or action.

In the year he relinquished his fellowship (1848) he published his first major poem, "The Bothie of Tober-na-Vuolich".[3] It is major in length and, despite its air of lightheartedness, full of insight and vitality, a kind of novel in verse, vivid with characterisation that makes it extremely readable. Clough was almost thirty when it was published. It introduces his most fecund period, over by the time he was thirty-five. It is written in hexameters, and adopts a flexible, colloquial approach to its love story, based on a reading party of undergraduates with their Tutor in the Scottish Highlands. It swells out into some remarkable passages of water symbolism (that suggest that in Clough we might have had a Swinburne before his time) in which sexual passion and response to it are imaged in terms of seas and burns in a compelling surge, cf. Section VII, circa lines 101-146, eg.:

> You are too strong Mr Philip. I am but a poor slender burnie,
> Used to the glens and the rocks, the rowan and birch of the woodies,
> Quite unused to the great salt sea; quite afraid and unwilling,"
> (115-7)

> And the passion she just had compared to the vehement ocean,
> Urging in high spring-tide its masterful way through the mountains,
> Forcing and flooding the silvery stream, as it runs from the inland;
> That great power withdrawn, receding here and passive,
> Felt she in myriad springs ...
> With a blind forefeeling descending ever, and seeking ...
> (135-139, 143)

There is pulse, incident, zest, and Clough's doubts are given a rest. The freedom and change of environment and, to an extent, of language, and some happy encounter perhaps, freed his imagination, while a sense of release at having made his decision to give up his Fellowship may have played its part. It is full of that "buoyant and exultant energy" R H Hutton has identified. Natura Naturans", written a couple of years earlier and published in *Ambarvalia* (with his friend Thomas Burbidge) in 1849, has much in common with it. Again there is an unexpected affinity with Swinburne in the poem's sustained energy and luxurious natural imagery. It got a bad notice in the *Literary Review* of 1849 and his widow did not include it in her posthumous edition of her husband's works.

After some uncertainties as to his religious position, early in 1849, he was appointed Principal of the University of London's Hall in Gordon Square - the building which now houses Dr William's Library. There were to be similar problems to those he had had over the Articles, but he was not due to take up his duties till October, so he took himself off to Rome from April to June, at the crux of Republican feeling and when Rome was under siege by French troops. The experience produced his other major poem, again in hexameters, again a novel in verse, but this time a story of a relationship in letters, "Amours de Voyage", written in Rome, at the height of the fighting, but not published until 1858. In the context of his *creative* career, however, it is logical to consider it at this juncture. The "Bothie" was youthful and ardent' "Amours de Voyage", written in Rome, though drafted only a year or so later, is elegant, subtle, witty with, as a contrast, the love theme unfulfilled. Yet there is the same energy; the same readability:

Canto III: I: Mary Trevellyn to Miss Roper:

... it is but when he talks of ideas
That he is quite unaffected, and free, and expansive, and easy;
...
She that should love him must look for small love in return, - like the ivy
On the stone wall, must expect but a rigid and niggard support, and
E'en to get that must go searching all round with her humble embraces.

Canto IV: I: Claude to Eustace:

Gone from Florence; indeed! and that is truly provoking; –
Gone to Milan, it seems; then I go also ...
Why, what else should I do? Stay here and look at the pictures ...?

Canto V: XI: Mary Trevellyn to Miss Roper:

Oh, and you see I know so exactly how he would take it:
Finding the chances prevail against meeting again, he would banish
Forthwith every thought of the poor little possible hope, which
I myself could not help, perhaps, thinking only too much of ... [4]

Insight, there, as well as entertainment from one who is perhaps less important as the embattled Victorian thinker of his image, than as a sensitive, almost too comprehensive intelligence, able to discern and to express the feelings of men and women in a manner far in advance of his age. It is that; the energy of his feeling for and expression of life, and packing a great deal of it into a few lines, that gives his work enduring force and attractiveness, and its relevance to our own day; true as it is, that we share his doubts too. The fact that he also wrote the well-known "Say not the struggle naught availeth", quoted by Winston Churchill in a broadcast of 1941, does not in itself prove this assertion wrong. The latter, his most famous piece, was drafted during the siege of Rome in 1849, at the same time as "Amours de Voyage", with "Peschiera" to follow:

Tis better to have fought and lost,

Than never to have fought at all. (1850)

Back at University Hall in London, after his extended and fruitful time in Italy, the old problem returned. For one thing he was rather lonely, though friends like Palgrave, then vice principal to Frederick Temple, at Kneller Hall, visited him or wrote. It is understandable that a man reluctant to attend the statutory prayers might endanger his position and perhaps he should never have accepted the post which Crabb Robinson and James Martineau had helped to secure for him. Pressure on him increasing, and thinking that a post of classics professor at Sydney would be his, he handed in his resignation in January 1852. The post at Sydney did not materialise yet in June he became engaged to Blanche Mary Shore Smith, daughter of Samuel Smith, an Examiner of Private Bills, of Coombe Hurst, Kingston Hill, Surrey. Blanche was a cousin of Florence Nightingale, an apparent footnote that will prove of significance. Unable to decide how to earn the £500 - £600 a year that Mr Smith insisted upon before marriage, Clough took himself off to America where he was received warmly by Emerson, Longfellow, J R Lowell, Charles Eliot Norton and Harriet Beecher Stowe. He took a few private pupils; got involved in a translation of Plutarch; thought about opening a school, but with characteristic indecision did nothing about it. The voyage out had produced the "Songs of Absence", several of which have a beautiful control of expression and an emotion under full ironic control. Citation of some first lines serves to indicate their clarity and appeal:

Where lies the land to which the ship would go?

Come home, come home, and where is home for me?

That out of sight is out of mind ...

Were you with me, or I with you ...

As on earlier occasions, and again as with Swinburne, intriguingly, anything to do with water or the sea seems to turn on some fecund poetic valve. Even "Dipsychus", one of his few other extended, multi-faceted efforts, unfinished as it was at his death, had been drafted at Venice in 1850. One piece in it is extremely well-known:

As I sat at the cafe, I said to myself,
They may talk as they please about what they call pelf, ...
How pleasant it is to have money, heigh ho!
How pleasant it is to have money.

Was he to stay in America or return to England? The question could not be put by, but he did procrastinate over it. Should he accept an Examinership in the Education Office in London; stay in America, possibly starting a school, or accept a post at Kneller Hall, offered by Temple, who exercised immense patience and kindness as Clough twisted and turned hoping for someone other than himself to make the decision. The tortuous story which must have left all concerned limp, not least Blanche and her father, can be traced in Clough's correspondence.[5] It begins with a letter from Temple of 10th May 1853 in which he explains that there are six Clerkships in the Education Office, beginning at 300 and rising by 25 per annum to 600, and that the Ashburtons and Lingen have arranged for Lord Granville to offer him a place, and that they and Temple advise him to accept. On the other hand, Palgrave would be prepared to take that job, and allow Clough to come to Kneller Hall where he could start at 400 rising in three years to 500. Temple ends: "I should be glad of a very speedy reply. Perhaps you will bring the reply in person." Through letters 367 to 390, exchanged between all manner of parties, the issue tossed itself about across the Atlantic till on the 28th June it appears that he *will return* but only because Temple and Blanche have virtually accepted the Examinership for him. He did accept the post, and duly married Blanche Smith in June of the following year, 1854. From that moment his poetry appears to have dried up, till a mild resurgence, right at the end of his life, 6-7 years later, when he was ill and travelling abroad for his health. The marriage had issue and his daughter Blanche Athena was to write the life of his sister, Anne Jemima. His wife, Blanche Mary, had much to contend with, however, quite apart from the uncertainties of their courtship during his absence in America. Now that she was married, "The Lady with the Lamp" was the problem. Florence Nightingale's own biographer was to write: "Blanche's life had been broken up by Florence's absorption of Clough. For the past year Blanche had been living with her children in her father's house, while Clough stayed in London."[6] In October 1854 he escorted Florence as far as Calais, on her way to the Crimea. In 1855 he was involved in controversial correspondence on her behalf. Gradually he became her unofficial dogsbody, as well as secretary to the Trustees of the Nightingale Fund. Often, after a tiring day's work, he would be summoned away to wait upon her in Hampstead. If there was emotional involvement on either side, it was not in any dishonourable sense, though she was still a beautiful woman at the time he first met her. To her the "cause" was everything, and she made the same demands on everyone. Sidney Herbert, the War Minister, was harassed to death by her and his wife working in unison. She turned on her Aunt Mai, when she felt she had to put her family first after devoting years to Florence's concerns. Clough we may suppose, like Sidney Herbert, was a willing volunteer, who found in her altruistic work, something worthwhile, and that served to anoint his exertions. He may have been glad to involve himself in practical issues of which he could not doubt the value however remote from the sphere of his own personal gifts. Possibly, too, there was a welcoming of, a need of, outside or "higher" authority, a touch of masochism even, in the psychological sense,[7] as in the difficulty of reaching a decision over marriage and job when in America. It was an escape from those wrestlings with truth, belief, purpose, his scruples over the Articles which had so distracted his energies, yet had coincided with his main years of poetic activity. It is like the arbitrary Medici rule in Florence which produced wonderful art. Unrest is not a desirable state, in itself, yet it may coincide with creativity in a way that more settled, worthy periods may not, and this is true for individuals as for nations. He had probably given up on the deep questions and his poetry, consciously or not, before he became involved with Florence's work. Yet there seems little doubt but that his subservient labours, coming on top of his examinership duties, wantonly taxed his constitution, and militated against imaginative and literary pursuits. By the end of 1859 he was overtaxed. In December he had scarlatina. In summer 1860 he broke his toe and was down in health generally. Herbert Spencer meeting him that autumn discerned physical and mental weariness, close to exhaustion. By 1861 he had to take leave from his work and travel in Europe seeking restoration. It separated him from Blanche, who was expecting a child, but spared him Florence's exactions. It was now, significantly, that he began to work on some narrative poems, since for so long he'd simply not had the mental space to do so. "Mari Magno", while not his best work, shows some return of his creative enthusiasms. They are tales of the sort we associate with Victorian novels - disloyalties or temptations, with the emphasis on the story and with character and motive assessments on the sympathetic side. But there is not the gusto or wit of his best earlier work, though the "Currente calamo" passage in "My Tale" paints a delightful picture and is as emotionally honest as ever.

He died in Florence, probably of a stroke, on 13th November 1861, Blanche having been able to join him for the last few weeks. Sidney Herbert had died in the August of the same year, slated by Florence for abandoning the cause dear to them both. Blanche held Forence partly responsible for her husband's death, and with reason. Francis Newman (brother of the Cardinal) seems to have taken that view. In Liz Herbert's case, she herself had seemed to abet Florence's worst exactions. Clough was buried in the Protestant cemetery in Florence, ironically in view of F.N.'s name and birthplace. Some seven years later Matthew Arnold published his pastoral elegy "Thyrsis", a "monody" to commemorate his friend. Keatsian pastiche as some consider it, it remains to many a particularly beautiful and moving poem; of almost equal merit to "The Scholar Gipsy" with its similarities of scene and mood. Arnold evokes Clough's questing spirit with great finesse, but perhaps makes too much of his religious and intellectual unease (doubless because Arnold shared it) and indecisive melancholy (doubtless because, industrious as he was, he feared the canker of the same characteristics within his own spirit). It is thus true that Arnold has to be held partially responsible for the received view of Clough as an ineffectual aspirer, not quite able to cope. But there are some wonderful verses, which Clough inspired; descriptions of Oxford and the country round it:

> And that sweet city with her dreaming spires,
> She needs not June for beauty's heightening.
>
> I know what white, what purple fritillaries
> The grassy harvest of the river-fields,
> Above by Ensham, down by Sandford, yields,
> And what sedg'd brooks are Thames's tributaries

or the verses beginning "So some tempestuous morn in early June" and "Too quick despairer, wherefore wilt thou go?; and the evocation of that temper of Clough's spirit, paralleled in many Victorian minds:

> It irked him to be here, he could not rest ...
> Some life of men unblessed
> He knew, which made him droop, and filled his head
>
> And long the way appears, which seem'd so short
> To the unpractised eye of sanguine youth;
> And high the mountain-tops, in cloudy air,
> The mountain-tops where is the throne of Truth
>
> A fugitive and gracious light he seeks,
> Shy to illumine; and I seek it too.
> This does not come with houses or with gold,
> With place, with honour, and a flattering crew;
> 'Tis not in the world's market bought and sold,
> But the smooth slipping weeks
> Drop by, and leave its seeker still untired;
> Out of the heed of mortals he is gone,
> He wends unfollow'd, he must house alone;
> Yet on he fares, by his own heart inspired.

It is true. He wore himself out seeking for truth and refusing to compromise; then he did compromise, as it must have seemed to him, in taking the Examinership, though it is hard to see what else he could or, indeed, ought to have done. And the knowledge that he had compromised, taken in conjunction with his overwork (albeit that it was in altruistic service) crushed his last resources. It all told against the joyous, natural current of his gift. His poetry of the heart endures, however, and is both varied and original.It includes two major achievements, that retain their stature and accessibility: the "Bothie" with its zest and happy ending; "Amour de Voyage", with its colloquial wit and understanding, its elegance, a story of missed opportunities. Both poems show new, and disarming, ways of writing pieces of length and ambition. Both poems show understanding of feminine as well as masculine psychology. The "Songs of Absence" contain some beautiful, clear cut lyrics; "Natura Naturans" and "Currente Calamo" are also lyrical and direct, yet set up intriguing reverberations, especially the former. The final "Mari Magno" narratives, in pentameter couplets, show in their different manner the same concern with human nature and motive as do the two major poems. For any life, let alone one that barely exceeded forty years, it is a legacy of substance, and one that retains the verve of its input. Yet there is something in Clough which it is not easy to encapsulate. It is that gifted idealism we see in Coleridge that, capable of so much, scarcely knows what to do, or whether what it does is worth the doing; or what to do first. So like Coleridge, he did seem to leave behind him less than that of which he had appeared capable. It is a question of that religious concern; indeed, that fervour of concern, which, allied with uncertainty and scrupulosity, he shared with so many sensitive minds of his age. It is that quality which his friends struggled to put into words; the sense of a questing, restless spirit, almost too "conscious" and conscientious, altogether too sensitive, for our rough world that calls for action; a conscience that would not let him excape from its conclusions; yet an intellectual elegance and subtlety, too, a zest for life that is too often hidden from us, and a partial acceptance of uncertainties that makes him akin to our late twentieth-century selves, heirs as we are of Kierkegaard and Wittgenstein. His friends leave us a haunting feeling of what they felt he might have achieved. One imagines they felt that something in him had died before his body did. His schooling, with all its rigours; the expectations that were entertained for him; his family's absence in America at a formative period, the need to accept the Examinership, Florence Nightingale's exactions, it all combined to reduce his oeuvre and its afflatus, and to break the man, but never completely. Impulse had been stifled in him, yet he remained a highly subtle and adult narrator of the heart's affections. Perhaps he should have written novels, but "Amours de Voyage" *is* one, really. It is more justification for a life than running errands for Florence Nightingale, one might suggest, if provocatively, but he did both; and for that the sick and infirm, as well as readers of books and scholars of literature, can remain grateful.[8]

Notes
1 Katherine Chorley: *Clough: the uncommitted mind*, 1962
2 There are parallels with Housman, here, who failed through emotional difficulties, and had to spend years in the wilderness, doubtless distorting his nature further in the process.
3 A "bothie" is a hut or humble dwelling.
4 *Selected Poems*; ed. Shirley Chew. Carcanet/Fyfield, 1987, an edition to be commended; Poems ed. F T Palgrave, with a memoir, Macmillan, 1862; *Selections from the Poems*; ed. Blanche Clough, 1894, and her earlier: *Poems and prose remains*, 2v., 1869.
5 *The Correspondence of Arthur Hugh Clough*; ed. F Mulhauser, Clarendon Press, 1957.
6 Cecil Woodham-Smith: *Florence Nightingale*, Constable, 1950, 330
7 "The spirit of service" might be a better term for it, lest the parallel with Swinburne be taken too far.
8 Based on a lecture given at the National Portrait Gallery on 30th June, 1993.

7. ARNOLD

In his *Victorian Anthology* (1902), Grant Duff, the typical, cultured public man of his day, sometime Governor of Madras, MP and friend of Gladstone, includes some dozen poems by Arnold, a proportion only equalled by Browning and Tennyson; Clough, Faber, Keble and Lord Lytton being at the next level of favour. Arnold has traditionally placed third in any evaluation (or "batting average") of Victorian poets, though nowadays Swinburne and Hopkins, besides Clough, Rossetti and Hardy, could be seen to make a strong claim, taking Yeats as of the twentieth century. Arnold was a Romantic who came to deny his Romanticism - as did Eliot, Pope, and Clough a little. But in his lifetime, as for many readers still today, his poems expressed the religious strains and uncertainties of the age for many earnest and reflective spirits subject to loss of confidence and focus. "Dover Beach", whatever its original inspiration, is indeed so used by a recent writer.[1] Other readers have simply enjoyed for their own sake poems such as "Thyrsis" or "The Scholar Gipsy", with their evocations of Oxford and Thames-side scenery, though there, too, the elegiac note and consciousness of this "strange disease of modern life" with its "sick hurry, its divided aims", is very evident . On hearing of Arnold's death, Grant Duff said: "to me his poems say more than those of any other poet who has lived in our time."

Matthew Arnold (1822-1888) was born at Laleham, near Staines, on Christmas Eve, 1822. His father was the formidable Dr Arnold, the ethical, aspiring headmaster of Rugby, who died in 1842, in his mid-forties. His mother was Mary Penrose. He had two brothers. One, Tom, like Matthew a friend of Clough, taught and inspected in Tasmania and New Zealand, before becoming Professor of English Literature at Dublin. The other, William Delafield, became an assistant commissioner in the Punjab; was invalided home, and died at Gibraltar in 1859. Tom's daughter Mary became Mrs Humphrey Ward, author of *Robert Elsmere* – a novel about religious integrity, significantly - and influential in the founding of the Mary Ward settlement in London. Matthew was very conscious of his own lack of achievement, as he saw it, and of not holding any post commensurate with his gifts or background. He could not help comparing himself with his father and brothers and joked about the servants' hall being the right place for him if he paid a social visit. True he became a Professor of Poetry at Oxford (1857-67) and lectured subsequently in America, but his principal career, that of an inspector of schools, was to prove his administrative competence rather than provide a proper sphere for the poet placed so highly in the pantheon of his peers, or the critic who T S Eliot regarded as one of our literature's major figures. But if circumstance or predilection was to lead him to surrender his imaginative lyric impulses at a sadly early age, he produced certain wistful poems that readers of several generations have taken to their hearts. In elegiac mode he is always moving and has few equals. Hopkins was to speak of him as "a rare genius and a great critic" and Walter Bagehot took his poems with him on his honeymoon. So treasure was laid up, before his Muse was packed off or wilted away.

In 1830 he returned to Laleham as pupil of his maternal uncle, the Revd. John Buckland. In August 1836 he went to Winchester and in 1837 to Rugby where, as later at Oxford, he produced prize poems. In 1841 he followed Clough to Balliol, to which he had won a classical scholarship. They became close friends, sharing the struggle between contending codes and bureaucracies of belief; the struggle between ethical and aesthetic impulses, the life of feeling as against the application of mind and will. At Oxford he affected Dandyism and appeared to waste his time. Charlotte Bronte was one of the few to note the "real modesty" and "intellectual aspirations" below the "seeming foppery" and "assumed conceit". He did only get a second class degree but his first class response to Oxford is in his poems. In March 1845 he obtained a Fellowship at Oriel. After a brief time as a master at Rugby he became in 1847 private secretary to Lord Lansdowne and in 1851 an inspector of schools, a post he retained until his retirement in 1886. As in the case of his friends Palgrave and Clough, and so many others, such employment must diminish the scope of creative activity, depressing aspirations and atrophying talents that might otherwise find a much fuller realisation. However much good he like Clough did for his fellow citizens, the artistic loss cannot be hidden. The very background, expectations and education of these men worked against them producing original, vulnerable, volcanic, Dionysian work. It is true Hopkins managed it (his vows removing him from the public sphere) but most don't. You have to be on the fringe of a society, a Blake or a Browning, something of a Nonconformist. Yet the taste and mellow charm of "privilege" has its virtue, too. Take the story of his friend Frederick Temple (the future Archbishop) tutoring the affectedly idle Arnold for an examination; sitting up all night with him, explaining the principles of goemetry, while Arnold lay back in an armchair with closed eyes, only murmuring occasionally, "what wonderful fellows these Greeks were" and, needless to say, doing well next day. It is in his late twenties and early thirties that his poetry flowered. It was (mostly) published by the time he was thirty-five. There was a family home at Fox How, near Ambleside, that with the associations of Oxford and the Thames, and his visits to France and Switzerland, contributed to his poetry, along with his friends and his reading. In Thun, Switzerland, he met a blue-eyed Marguerite, of whom we know little, except the lyrics entitled "Switzerland" that she inspired. There is the lovely first paragraph of "Parting" and the fine lyrical effusion that concludes with its significant: "Forgive me! forgive me!" and "In the void air, towards thee,/ My stretch'd arms are cast;/ But a sea rolls between us -/ Our different past." And the marvellous, if bathetically titled, "To Marguerite - Continued" with its "unplumbed, salt, estranging sea." Whether he abandoned her or she him will never be known. But I suspect that he abandoned what she represented, anyhow; that he denied some inner conviction or impulse that haunted him ever afterwards and dried him up. That well-known and beautiful poem "The Forsaken Merman" doubtless bears on these matters. It has an inner consistency and pulse (assisted by judicious repetitions) that make it one of his finest. In 1851 he married Frances Lucy Wightman, daughter of a Queens Bench judge; took the inspectorate and settled to the grindstone. He subdued himself to the mood of one "who saw life steadily, and saw it whole", as he writes in his sonnet "To a Friend", and his Muse beats vainly against that calm stoicism, that "victorious brow" that he admires in his sonnet on "Shakespeare". Yet in the firm control of these pieces, as in the compassion of his "East London" "West London" sonnets, there speaks the toiler who strove to improve English education and the uncle of Mary (Mrs Humphrey Ward).

His first book of poems "The Strayed Reveller" appeared in 1849, giving only the intial "A" as its author. 500 copies were printed but it was withdrawn before many were sold. It included "Mycerinus" and "The Forsaken Merman" and ends with "Resignation", a poem stoic in mood yet possessed of a sturdy rhythm and evocative power that recalls such rambles to at least one reader. It looks back to Wordsworth yet forward, in certain respects, to the more positive Yeats:

    ... the mute turf we tread
    The solemn hills around us spread ...
    If I might lend their life a voice,
    Seem to bear rather than rejoice.

1852 saw the publication of "Empedocles on Etna", again giving "A" as its author. The title poem includes the song of Callicles, the harp-player, and like the narrative poem "Tristram and Iseult" has passages of great beauty within the framework of a longer poem. This 1852 volume was followed by extended re-arrangements between 1853 and 1857 which seemed to indicate the onset of a great poetic career. But it had already touched its peaks, and only a handful of fine things were to follow. In the *Poems* of 1853, "Sohrab and Rustrum" on classical models, with its fine ending commencing "But the majestic river floated on", and the elegiac, wistfully ideal "Scholar Gipsy" were outstanding additions. The worthy "Balder Dead" was added in 1855, but this, like "Sohrab and Rustrum" is written in a style, and on a subject, alien to the temper of an age to which the poetry of Milton (say) is practically a dead book. To his still-born drama "Merope" (1858) this comment particularly applies. More to the point is the elegiac lyric "A Southern Night" written in memory of his brother William Delafield Arnold who died at Gibraltar, and his sister-in-law. There is life, verbal and evocational, in the very first words: "The sandy spits, the shore-locked lakes,/ Melt into open, moonlit sea", that is at a far remove from the glum classical exercises into which he could lapse, and there is, in the allusive use of proper names and invocations of far flung places, an anticipation of Housman:[2]

> Ah me! Gibraltar's strand is far,
> But further yet across the brine
> Thy dear wife's ashes buried are,
> Remote from thine.
>
> For there, where morning's sacred fount
> It's golden rain on earth confers,
> The snowy Himalayan Mount
> O'ershadows hers. ...

Time and again he responds to elegiac impulse, reminding us of the characteristic threnodies of our literature, "Lycidas", Henry King's "Exequy on his Wife", "Ave atque Vale" and "Adonais". "The Scholar Gipsy" is an "ideal" elegy; an elegy in every sense but the literal, and worthy surely of its illustrious peers:

> Still nursing the unconquerable hope,
> Still clutching the inviolable shade,
> With a free, onward impulse brushing through,
> By night, the silver'd branches of the glade ...

Quite different is the elegy "Rugby Chapel" written on the death of his father. Dr Arnold died in 1842 but Arnold did not write the poem until 1857. It is restrained, with many hesitations, stops, and changes of direction, and without rhyme; yet most moving. "Thyrsis" on the death of Clough was also some time in the maturing. Clough died in 1861 but the haunting sequel to, and fellow of, "The Scholar Gipsy" did not appear till 1867.[3] "Dover Beach" perhaps his best known poem, was published in 1867 but probably drafted about 1851, at the time of his marriage, or as early as 1848, in which case it could relate to Marguerite. It could tie in with the poems headed "Faded Leaves" which are not far from the mood of the "Switzerland" sequence:

> So far apart their lives are thrown
> From the twin soul which halves their own. ("Too Late")

– or the song-like pathos of "Longing". The little he wrote hereafter tends to be reflective, mildly melancholy, with little sign of the early deep, ordered feeling.

Why did Arnold dry up as a poet? There are several possible explanations, any one or two of which might do: (1) that he wrote the lyric poetry which came to him, and had more integrity than to pretend to it when it wasn't there; (2) that his insistence on poetry having *use*; on its being (in his own words) "a criticism of life"; his belief in classical models and in seeing life "steadily", all worked against spontaneity and lyric utterance; (3) that his taste, his position, his prominence, the expectations had of him, imposed barriers and inhibitions which he lacked the force to overcome, with something of the same effect that we find in the cases of Palgrave and Clough; (4) that his heavy programme of work as a school inspector, the journeying, the examining, the report-writing, squeezed his inspiration dry and took its toll of energy and time (yet against this it could be argued that a poem is more likely to find its way up to the surface than the books he *did* write, which required a good deal of time and application; (5) that his wish to write poetry had waned, starved by something lacking in his emotional life. His parting from Marguerite, whether or not it was a denial on *his* part, may have had something to do with it. He may have denied the genuine response of the heart, though some of the lyrics we have quoted give embodiment to it. It may also have been a religious drying up; not of ethics, or commitment, necessarily, but of the flame that gives life to the wick. He himself felt the "dryness", and blamed his daily work, while finding value in what he could achieve through it. But he must have felt it to be a second best. In a letter to his mother as early as 1860 he writes: "with the limited sphere of action in outward life, which I have, what is life unless I occupy it in this manner, and keep myself from feeling starved and shrunk up?"; (6) that his work prevented him enjoying that occasional "freedom" or "fallowness" essential to any creative artist; a denial of the opportunity for lone musing which can be deadening, just as all absence from affairs can be deadening, too. In 1863 he writes to his wife: "we strolled back from Grantchester by moonlight; it made me melancholy to think how at one time I was in the fields every summer evening of my life, and now it is such a rare event to find myself there", and this when he was just into his forties. So we may add (7) that separation from the countryside could have been fatal to his inner well-being; certainly, to his poetry, for he rarely wrote of the town, as Eliot, Henley or Masefield sought to do, except in a sonnet or two.

In 1857 he was elected Professor of Poetry at Oxford, an appointment he retained for ten years. He did not teach or reside and carried on with his inspectorate, but in connection with his tenure he published two series of lectures: " On Translating Homer" (1861-2) and the distinctive series "On the Study of Celtic Literature", published in 1867, an imaginative choice of subject:

> The Celt's quick feeling for what is noble and distinguished gave his poetry style; his indomitable personality gave it pride and passion; his sensitivity and nervous exaltation gave it ... the gift of rendering with wonderful felicity the magical charm of nature, The forest solitude, the bubbling spring, the wild flowers, are everywhere in romance. They ... are nature's own children ... something quite different from the woods, waters and plants of Greek and Latin poetry ... Magic is just the word for it - the magic of nature; not merely the beauty of nature ... but the intimate life of nature, her weird power and her fairy charm ... (even to)

Gwydion wants a wife for his pupil: "Well", says Math, "we will seek, I and thou, by charms and illusions, to form a wife for him out of flowers. So they took the blossoms of the oak, and the blossoms of the broom, and the blossoms of the meadow-sweet, and produced from them a maiden, the fairest and most graceful that man ever saw. and they baptised her and gave her the name of Flower-Aspect.

Of course, we discern that Arnold is not so at home as in his more familiar classical fields, but somehow he gets to the imaginative truth of his subject and arouses our interest. If "Flower-Aspect" makes us think of the Japanese, there is affinity also with the flower references that give "The Scholar Gipsy" and "Thyrsis" so much of their homely appeal, and keep the poems rooted in earth. Yet there is something else in the passage. Arnold had what is "noble and distinguished" in his make-up in abundance, but isn't that "pride and passion", that "nervous exaltation" that he finds in the Celt, exactly what he came to lack? Yet he was not without an impulsive quirk of humour. The D.N.B. tells us that certain of his lectures were "disfigured by inexcusable flippancies at the expense of persons entitled to the highest respect." Yet in the same place, these lectures are termed "a classic of criticism."[4]

"Essays in Criticism" his critical essays and lectures, appeared from 1865 till his death; his approach showing a mind both highly ordered and highly concerned, a little like George Steiner's in our own day. With Ruskin and Carlyle, with whom he shares occasionally an exhortatory tone, he raised the standards of criticism, brought to it intellect, learning, and (so far as he could) objectivity, and proved something of a founding father to the criticism that would come after him. 1859 saw a pamphlet on "England and the Italian question." He travelled on the Continent in connection with his duties and produced reports such as "The Popular Education of France", "A French Eton", "Schools and Universities on the Continent", all dating from the 1860's. They are conscientious, interesting, useful in their day - but it is a pity their subjects could not have been more literary or enduring. Not that Arnold would have agreed necessarily. He liked to think that he was fulfilling some ethically and socially useful function and was concerned to see his poetry viewed in that light. Thus he was mightily pleased when Andrew Lang, in a review of 1882, said that it might "do more to cultivate the love of beauty and the love of nature, to educate and console, than many great volumes of theology." In his lectures he often rails against English apathy, as he saw it. He bravely criticised Lowe's Educational Code in 1862, when doing so might have affected his career but it was a different kind of courage, presumably, that caused him to make an unsuccessful application for the librarianship of the House of Commons. In 1858 he had taken root at 2 Chester Square, London, but moved to Harrow in 1868. The sad loss of three of his sons could itself bear on his poetry's mood and withering, as does the perception that his mind may have been more critical than constructive in temper; yet mood and withering were in evidence earlier.

than constructive in temper; yet mood and withering were in evidence earlier. In 1873 he moved to Pain's Hill, Cobham, Surrey and, in 1875, declined renomination for the Oxford Professorship of Poetry, in favour of his fellow Balliol alumnus and long-standing friend, Francis Turner Palgrave.

Culture and Anarchy, an essay in political and social criticism, as it is subtitled, appeared in 1869; *St Paul and Protestantism* in 1870. The first is an important work, but uneven, and in neither is he at his best. He pursues his attack on English society's Philistian elements, as he saw them, using a good deal of heavy irony and arguments that are, occasionally, unsustainable, as when, in his structures on Puritans and dissenters he contends that "the Puritans are, and always have been, deficient in the specifically Christian sort of righteousness".[5] This intriguing view does appear to lack that courtesy and reasonableness normally to be associated with the believer in "sweetness and light" and seeing life "steadily" and "whole", and it recalls those comments of Kingsley which provoked Newman's masterly *Apologia Pro Vita Sua* in reply. There is point in some of his arguments, though it is hardly tenable to deny dissenters access to higher education, as was the case for so many years and then, in effect, to accuse them of not possessing the culture it gives. But we may all err outside our own field or when writing under pressure of time, age, or *geist*, *zeit* or otherwise.

In 1883 he received through Gladstone a Civil List pension, though he did not retire until 1886. In the winter of 1883 he undertook a lecture tour in America, his eldest daughter having settled there on marriage; and in 1886 he undertook a further series. A few, very few poems emerged occasionally, two on dogs, one on a canary. By far the most important, in which his elegiac gift did glow again, if fitfully, is the uneven "Westminster Abbey", occasioned by the death of its Dean, Arthur Stanley in 1881:

Rough was the winter eve;
Their craft the fishers leave,
And down over the Thames the darkness drew.
One still lags last, and turns, and eyes the Pile
Huge in the gloom, across on Thorney Isle ...
His mates are gone, and he
For mist can scarcely see
A strange wayfarer coming to his side ...

The beginning is the best of it but I won't quote (out of context) the exordium's climactic finest lines; albeit their virtue is narrative, intrinsically, rather than technical.

Toward the end of 1885 he was abroad again, on behalf of the Royal Commission on Education. In 1886 he reported on his tour of elementary education in Germany, Switzerland and France. So it was that, almost all his adult life, he lived two careers, and mixed literature with arduous educational was published posthumously. So if, indeed, fit only for the servants' hall, as he had jested, he had proved a faithful servant to his country, a patriot truly. In *A French Eton* (1864) he had written these words in seeking to realise his aim of a "cultured, liberalized, ennobled, transformed middle class":

> Children of the future, whose day has not yet dawned, you, when that day arrives, will hardly believe what obstructions were long suffered to prevent its coming! You ... whose power of simple enthusiasm is your great gift, will not comprehend how progress toward man's best perfection - the adorning and ennobling of his spirit - should have been reluctantly undertaken; how it should have been ... retarded by barren commonplaces, by worn-out clap-traps.

There speaks one worthy to be numbered, surely, with W E Forster, the Quaker who promoted the Elementary Education Act of 1870; Ruskin and Carlyle, and the Newman of *The Idea of a University* who toiled in Dublin, and many a less known figure like the father of technical education Thomas Twining and the Baptist John Clifford. There speaks a worthy son of Dr Arnold, in whose shadow he must have spend his every day. He and Palgrave both had "strong" fathers, and it cannot have been all that easy for them. He died in Liverpool on April 18th 1888, hastening to meet his daughter who was visiting from America, and he was buried at Laleham, in the place where he was born. Friends of the composer Borodin hoped he might be ill, so that he could compose instead of being engaged in chemistry. So we might regret that Arnold was not sick more often, so that we might have heard more "ignorant armies clash by night" ("Dover Beach"); more of the "world applaud the hollow ghost/ Which blamed the living man" ("Growing Old"); seen more of the "high Midsummer pomps come on" and "the musk carnations break and swell" ("Thyrsis"); more of the "moonlit pales" ("The Scholar Gipsy"); and gone down once more "down, down down!/ down to the depths of the sea!" ("The Forsaken Merman").

Elegiac poet par excellence, he recognised, as we do that:

Though the Muse be gone away,
Though she move not earth today,
Souls erewhile who caught her word,
Ah! still harp on what they heard.[6,7.]

Notes
1 Cf. *The Sea of Faith* by Don Cupitt, (BBC, 1984) which takes its title from Arnold's poem.
2 Proper names are not the only connection with Housman; cf the relevance of "The Last Word" cited in the Housman chapter and Housman's appreciation of Arnold as a critic.
3 Quoted in the chapter on Clough above, and like "The Scholar Gipsy", in "Keatsian" stanzas.
4 The reference is to the series on translating Homer.
5 Cited by Donald Davie in his *A Gathered Church*, 1978, 80-81
6 The grimly-titled "Persistence of Poetry"; the whole poem is quoted.
7 Based on a lecture given at the National Portrait Gallery, 19th April 1994

8. PALGRAVE

Francis Turner Palgrave (1824-1897), the "Golden Treasury" man, was born at Great Yarmouth on 28th September 1824. He was the eldest of four brothers, all of whose names appear in the record books[1], son of Sir Francis Palgrave[2], the historian, and Elizabeth, daughter of Dawson Turner, a partner in the bank of Gurney & Co. His paternal grandfather was Meyer Cohen, a Jewish stockbroker of Kentish Town, Sir Francis having changed his name on marriage. Sir Francis was an historian specialising in Anglo-Norman history; "he *worked*" as John Murray once put it to the writer, and became deputy-keeper of the public records; cultivated the Murray of his day (publisher of Scott and Byron), compiled the first edition of Murray's *Handbook for Travellers in Northern Italy*, contributed to the Quarterly Review and translated a paper by Ugo Foscolo, the Italian patriot and poet.

The poet's childhood was spent in Great Yarmouth, Westminster and Hampstead Green, where the family moved in 1832. His early friends included the Aldersons (cf. "To G.C.A.") and the Gurneys (with their banking and Quaker connections) both of whom had East Anglian roots, and Blanche Mary Shore Smith, later the wife and, all too soon, the widow of Arthur Hugh Clough. Educated privately till the age of 14, he entered the Charterhouse in 1838, then still at its Charterhouse Square site, close to the Barbican station. He and his brother Gifford used to catch the stage to school in the morning and walk back up to Hampstead Green in the evening. In July 1838 he was watching the Coronation of Victoria from John Murray's Albemarle Street windows. In July 1841 he saw the City elections at the Guildhall with the ballad-singers, bill-stickers, dense crowd, elbowing and bribery. It was a far cry from the cultured, studious atmosphere in which he was generally cloistered, with plenty of society but much study and reading, touring on the Continent, and informed interest in art. His father was much interested in art and his mother had had Cotman as a drawing master. His letters at this time make constant reference to art and architecture, and to his reading, especially the classical texts that formed a good part of his diet. In 1843, the year that he won a scholarship to Balliol, he went with his father to Rome, via Antwerp, the Rhine and Switzerland. At Balliol he made the friendships with Clough, Arnold, Shairp and Temple already touched on; also meeting Robert Morier (the future diplomat) and Archibald Peel, nephew of the statesman. His tutor was Benjamin Jowett. He heard Newman preach and was influenced by him. Pictures of the Madonna and Child hung on his walls. At Oxford he was also to meet Arthur (Dean) Stanley, cf. Arnold's poem at his death; J A Froude, Max Muller (Cf. Palgrave's sonnet to him "To M - M -")[3], and Sir Henry Acland. Early in 1846 he interrupted his studies to serve as assistant Secretary to Gladstone, then

Colonial Secretary. The hours of the office were from 11 to a little after 6, leaving him time for some reading, and he enjoyed the view over St James's Park. He obtained a First Class in Classics and in 1847 was elected a Fellow of Exeter College. In that year his brother Gifford, the adventurous one of the family (explorer, diplomat, missionary) with whom he had been very close, left for India, his grief being extreme.[4] In 1848 he visited Paris with Jowett, Arthur Stanley and Morier. It was at a turbulent time and several members of the party kept a journal of their visit. Dawson Turner offered to publish Palgrave's but Jowett and Stanley (each asked independently of the other) advised against it. Their own accounts were carefully preserved and appear in their biographies, but Palgrave's only survives (in part) in the life of Jowett. In a letter of April he writes of hearing the drum, and seeing the National Guard parading the streets; notes the few private carriages and misses "the old butterfly like sheen of brilliancy in the Gardens." In July Clough wrote to a friend: "Palgrave, you will have heard, has become, under Froude's guidance partly, and partly by revolutionary sympathy, a very suspect person at Oxford and next to myself is ... accounted the wildest ... republican going. I myself apropos of a letter of Matt's (Matthew Arnold's) which he directed to Citizen Clough, Oriel Lyceum, Oxford, bear the title par excellence ..."[5] Clough *was* joking, but it is certainly the decade following which saw a time of ferment for Palgrave, with the production of some of his most fervent work - little as this "ferment" may have been visible to the observer - before the world of taste rather than feeling closed in. On the surface at least he had to knuckle down and earn his living. In 1848 he entered the Education Department "Whitehall" (as distinguished from the Department of Science and Art "South Kensington") starting as an Assistant Examiner and becoming Assistant Secretary. His formative friendship with Tennyson dates from 31 March 1849, and before the end of April Tennyson was reading him some of the *In Memoriam* poems. This friendship, which meant much more to him than to Tennyson, was assisted when his work brought him near to Montpelier Row, Twickenham, where the older poet lived from 1851 to 1853.[6] From 1850 to 1855 he was vice-principal under Frederick Temple of the experimental college set up at Kneller Hall, on the Isleworth/Twickenham border, for the training of teachers of pauper and delinquent children. The high hopes entertained for this work, and the considerable effort that Temple (especially) put into it, were foiled by the half-heartedness of governments; the attitude of workhouse masters, and the lack of satisfactory practice schools or appropriate posts for the trained teachers to take up, with the result that the college was closed. As so often a splendid scheme was ill-backed and not followed through. Palgrave went back to "Whitehall", and Temple in due course became headmaster of Rugby. In 1850 Robert Peel had died and Palgrave wrote in his memory:

Too soon he purchased his enfranchisement:
He should have gone down to the grave in age.

Much as Palgrave deferred to Tennyson as a public figure, Swinburne much preferred his company to that of the Laureate (probably because his was the more accommodating nature) but then Swinburne couldn't stand the "Idylls of the King" and used to refer not to "Morte d'Arthur" but "Morte d'Albert". In 1852 Palgrave's mother had died. It was a loss that affected him deeply. As the eldest son, he now looked after his father and did not marry until after his death.

In 1854 Clough married Blanche and Palgrave, her "early playmate" published *Idyls and Songs*, following it in 1858 with his ardent, high-minded prose masterpiece *The Passionate Pilgrim* which, despite its quotations and elusive style, shows force of feeling, psychological understanding, and genuine if idealistic devotion. It was published under a pseudonym, but appears to date from 1854 and the Kneller Hall years. The poems in *Idyls and Songs* date from 1851 to 1854, mainly; to which can be added one or two appended to his *Lyrical Poems* of 1871, which he says were written between 1848 and 1854. So 1854 does seem to have been a culminating and critical year, and with other circumstantial evidence might suggest that Blanche Clough (née Smith) was the inspirer of these artefacts. The truth seems to be otherwise, however.[7] Briefly, the arguments in favour of another candidate are these:- His daughter says that he was a friend of Baron Alderson's children; they included not only Charles but Georgina Caroline Alderson (G.C.A.) (1827-1899) who was to marry Lord Robert Cecil, the future 3rd Marquis of Salisbury and Prime Minister on 11th July 1857. At the time of the wedding we find Charles writing: "My dear Frank, I feel sure that however deeply you are feeling the events of last Saturday week, it is not a subject which with me you would wish tabooed..." In October 1843, when he would have been just 19, he had spent two days with the Aldersons at Rickmansworth. In January of the following year he visited the British Museum with them and in 1846 he mentions that he had been at Norwich with the Aldersons. It is true she was three years younger but not purely an "early playmate" perhaps. It was nothing more than friendship at any time, on *her* part probably, but he was not the first (nor last) lover and lyric poet to feel himself somewhat more involved:

On that familiar scene, each other's mind,
There is no need for deep enquiring gaze:
No fear the trifles non-acceptance find
That confidence to confidence displays." ("To GCA" 12th April 1854)

There is heightened feeling in "Es Aei" though the actual words are conventional. We are worked on by the rhythmic thrust, the repetitions of refrain and rhyme, the potency of incantation so evident in the third verse:

By thy childhood's recollection,
By the truth of young affection,
By the love the years assure thee,
By thy sweet self I adjure thee -
Set the issue full before thee -
Can another so adore thee?
Hear my oath by all above thee
Past eternity to love thee." (September 1852)

In "Irony" (23 February 1853) the mood is darker in one sense; hope seems abandoned, yet there is more irony and control:

Yet 'neath this sovereign load of ill,
This vast inseparable regret,
The world maintains his tenour yet:-
Their tale of claims the days revive:-
– Not as we will,
But as we must we live.

A wry appreciation of the way even grief can pass is shown in "In Desiderium":

O thrice accurst - O worst than worst -
Past all despair's conceiving,
When 'tis not for the loss we grieve,
But for the loss of grieving (April 1853)

Yet in "L'Envoy" (27th March 1854) we find him sighing for:

The dear dear face I may not see
For evermore the dearest.

To set the relationship beyond doubt, Palgrave's own annotations in the British Museum copy of *Idyls and Songs* give "Alderson" against "To G.C.A." while "L'Envoy" refers back to "To G.C.A." In another copy he had pencilled against "L'Envoy": And much the young lady troubled her head about all this!" The good humour of such emotion recollected in tranquillity scarcely matches with his feeling at the time the poems were written, but Gwenllian records several visits of Palgrave and his wife to the Salisburys at Hatfield, which would accord with a reference of Brimley Johnson's to lifelong friendship. The mood of *The Passionate Pilgrim* is similar to that of the poems: "I looked round for miracles: I would have accepted omens ... and hoped that ... by the ordainment of chance or Providence, might be some elucidation of a future, in which I could discover no sign of happiness by the horoscopy of reason"[8.]

These books were published in his thirties; the texts probably written earlier. Thereafter we have a receding tide, except in one or two cases, hymns or otherwise. Much work is produced, but it is the work of periodical journalism, criticism, taste and opinion, the compilation of anthologies (a work of *taste* in itself), a book of tales for children, a book or two of essays, and poetry that fits a mind honed in his public school and Oxbridge classical tradition; a mind like Clough's and Arnold's, compelled to compromise with its feelings;

strained by the necessity to affect faith; constrained above all by the need to conform to position and expectation. It is significant that Clough, perhaps poetically the most gifted of the three, conformed comparatively the least (or stood out the longest) and produced (arguably) the most lively and original work. It is noteworthy that Palgrave both withdrew *Idyls and Songs* from circulation and gives scant sign of it in *Amenophis* (1892) said to contain "all he wished to preserve." If so it is an old man's choice; too safe a choice, and a pity, considering what is left out.

He had begun to contribute to the *Quarterly Review, Fine Arts Review, London Magazine*, and *Westminster Review*. Eventually these contributions would be collected in the *Essays on Art* of 1866 and elsewhere. In 1860 he toured Cornwall and the Scilly Isles with Tennyson and Holman Hunt, Thomas Woolner (sculptor and poet) and Val Prinsep, the painter and novelist. It was on this tour that the idea of his best known book *The Golden Treasury of the Best Songs and Lyrical Poems in the English Language* was born. The concept was a bold one, but there is no doubt that the achievement was on a par with it. Tennyson's judgments were formative but Palgrave's own taste and industry was crucial. It is sufficient testimony that the book has remained in print for so long a time, and was in use as a school textbook for a hundred years.[9] In the same year as its publication (1861) Palgrave's father died and Palgrave moved in with Woolner at 28 Welbeck Street. In the autumn of that eventful year came news of Clough's death in Florence. Whether he paid (or renewed) suit to Blanche, we do not know. He did edit Clough's poems in 1862, and provide a memoir, but (even with taste such as his) included one or two pieces that Blanche (for no very obvious reason) found too "warm". In the summer of 1862 he met Cecil Grenville Milnes-Gaskell, daughter of the MP for Much Wenlock; their engagement followed within a few weeks and on 30th December they were married at St Thomas's, Orchard Street, by W F Hook, Dean of Chichester (cf. a poem to him). They took up residence at 5 York Gate, moving some years later to 15 Chester Terrace, also on the edge of Regent's Park. In the evenings, after 8 hours work, he would pursue his art criticism or play duets for violin and piano with Cecil. In 1863 their first child, Cecil Ursula, was born, *The Times* crediting him with a daughter and *The Post* with a son. He had long known and admired many of the Pre-Raphaelites and their work and when in 1868 his delightful and unexpected *Five Days Entertainments at Wentworth Grange –* his stories for children on the five senses - was published, it had woodcuts by Arthur Hughes. About this time he brought out three small collections of hymns and a number of these remain in today's hymnbooks. Of these there are morning and evening hymns, of no great substance and the much more charged "Though we long, in sin-wrought blindness"; "Thou says'st, "Take up thy cross""[10], and "O Thou not made with hands" (or "The City of God") a favourite

49

of Archbishop Edward Benson.[11] Less suitable for congregational use is the powerful hymn of repentance ("When low ...") with its Crashaw-like colouring and force[12], alien to our age as it may be. In 1870 his infant son Arthur Frederick died and was buried in the cemetery on Barnes Common. In the following year his *Lyrical Poems* appeared, with its "Pro Mortuis" and its "At Lyme Regis", his first collection since the suppressed one of 1854, but by now he was nearly fifty.[13]

Cecil and he had spent a number of holidays at Lyme Regis and in 1872 he bought a house there. It was actually "two picturesque old gabled cottages, lately thrown into one, and the adjoining fields ... known since the time of Charles I as "Little Park"." The charm of the winding Haye Lane, with its several old cottages, its hedges and fine views, has survived to our own day, though somewhat threatened by modern development. In 1877 Palgrave stood for the Professorship of Poetry at Oxford but withdrew in favour of his friend Principal Shairp of Edinburgh, whom he had known in the "Balliol Scholar" days that Shairp commemorates. In 1878 Palgrave received the degree of LL.D. at Edinburgh. In 1880 there appeared the original "private" edition of *The Visions of England*, followed by the edition for general circulation of 1881. Dramatic and poignant poems combine with reflective and pastoral pieces to create a substantial, "nobly conceived sequence on British history", letters of appreciation being received from Longfellow, Lecky, J R Green, Sir Mountstuart Grant Duff,[14] and Henry James. There is an imaginative breadth and scope about it. It is ambitious and well-realised with its variety of mode in which vigorous ballad, lament, paean, joyful and sad pieces intermingle with quiet appreciation of the English countryside and its associations. It is a full-scale project and more accessible and readable than many that are better known. Contemporary history books and anthologies with some of its poems included can be found in antiquarian bookshops.[15] Whether or not - in conjunction with the inevitable lobbying – it helped to secure him the Poetry Professorship in 1885, it made the reward a deserved one.[16] He was elected with the support of Arnold, Tennyson and Browning, his chief rival, W J Courthope, being defeated by 60 votes. Palgrave served a five-year term and was then re-elected for a further five years. In 1887 his eldest daughter Cecil married James Duncan, Canon of Canterbury and Secretary of the National Society, Arnold and Browning signing the register. In the summer his *Ode* for Queen Victoria's Jubilee was published.[17] He visited Jowett at Balliol; spoke at Birmingham on "The Decline of Art" and visited Newman at the Oratory. He was impressed by the gentleness of the man he had heard preach so movingly so many years previously.

1888 saw the death of Arnold and of Palgrave's brother Gifford whose career has a glamour resembling Sir Richard Burton's and denied FTP. In 1889

Browning died, too. More heartening was the news that his *Treasury of Sacred Song* had sold out in four days. But in 1890, on 27th March, his wife, too, died. She was buried beside her infant son, in the cemetery on Barnes Common, kempt in 1984 but by 1996 in a bad state. Palgrave designed the cross which he erected to Cecil's memory in St Michael's churchyard at Lyme. He continued to visit Tennyson, though his arthritis must have made it a discomfort to travel, and took up metaphysics and astronomy. Tennyson died in 1892 and Palgrave contributed to Hallam Tennyson's biography of his father. *Amenophis and other poems* came out in 1892. The title poem, in three parts, in pentameter couplets, is concerned with the Exodus and the Greek, Egyptian and Jewish conception of God. There are sonnets to W F Hook and Wells & Severn, the "friends of young Keats'"; there are hymns and meditations. Perhaps the loveliest thing is "Autumn", however, first published in 1871, and worthy of Hardy or Housman, at their best:

With downcast eyes and footfall mild,
And close-drawn robe of lucid haze,
The rose-red Summer's russet child
O'er field and forest Autumn strays:
On lawn and mead at rising day
Tempers the green with pearly gray;
And 'neath the burning beech throws round
A golden carpet on the ground.

And oft a look of long regret
Her eyes to Summer's glory throw;
Delaying oft the brand to set
That strips the blossom from the bough:
And where in some low shelter'd vale
The last sweet August hues prevail,
Her eager frosts she will repress,
And spare the lingering loveliness.[18]

This poem, together with "Es Aei" and its fellows, a hymn or two, and the overall concept of *The Visions of England*, I number amongst his best achievements, whilst in prose, leaving aside his critical work, there are neglected riches in *The Passionate Pilgrim* and the *Wentworth Grange* tales, respectively. Some of the pastoral poems written around the Lyme area are also pleasing.

In 1895 he moved from Chester Terrace to a "smaller" house in Kensington, 15 Cranley Place. He was working on two books, both of which appeared in 1897, *Landscape in Poetry* based on lectures[19], and the second book (or "Second Series") of *The Golden Treasury*, dealing with the contemporary poets that he had omitted from his primary selection. Overall, for reasons discussed in the Appendix paper[20], it has never met with the favour accorded that of 1861. By the summer of 1897 his health had begun to decline. He was anxious, also, about his son who was working as a missionary in a remote part of British Columbia. It was fitting that he should live to have Hallam's life of Tennyson read to him, since his friendship with Tennyson was (for him) the dominating literary affection of his life. He died on 24th October 1897 and was buried beside his wife at Barnes. Frederick Temple read the burial service.

"I think I have loved truly: I struggled long: I have been corrected in anger, and brought to nothing", he says at the end of *The Passionate Pilgrim*. But are we to add, as he did: *"do manus*: it is in vain ..."?[21, 22]

Notes

1 The youngest or fourth son *Reginald Francis Douce* was Clerk to the House of Commons, KCB 1892, and author of books on Parliamentary practice. Reginald's daughter (and thus the poet's niece) Mary Elizabeth Palgrave (1858-1929) wrote children's stories such as *Under the Blue Flag* (SPCK) or *Between Two Opinions* one of several published by the Religious Tract Society.

The third son *Robert Harry Inglis* was a banker and political economist, editor of *The Dictionary of Political Economy* and initiator of a collected edition of his father's works.

The second son *William Gifford* was perhaps the most fascinating, gifted and, ultimately, thwarted, of all. Soldier, traveller, linguist, diplomat, author, priest. Broken in health he died as Minister Resident at Montevideo. His *Narrative of a Year's Journey through Central and Eastern Arabia* (1865) is still read. T E Lawrence once said: "Give due space to Palgrave and, if necessary, reduce the space on me."

2 Sir Francis Palgrave was born Cohen in 1788. *His* father Meyer Cohen, was a Jewish stockbroker of Kentish Town whose finances collapsed whilst Francis was still young, leaving him to make his own way in the world. He showed immense capacity and energy. He became a lawyer and a historian specialising in Anglo-Norman history. Cf. his *History of the Anglo-Saxons* reprinted 1989, and the rather appealing *The Merchant and Friar* of 1844, for example. At the end of his life (briefly) he was a Trustee of the National Portrait Gallery. He did valuable work in assembling and utilising documents. He was knighted in 1832. Through John Murray he got to know Dawson Turner, a banker at Great Yarmouth with cultivated tastes and a fine library, and a daughter Elizabeth (who became the poet's mother) of no mean ability or character. At one time she was a publisher's reader for Murray. Dawson Turner set him up financially; at the same time that Cohen changed his name and was baptised. The name Palgrave is Elizabeth's mother's maiden name. Letters from Francis and Elizabeth are included in the letters *The Palgraves to John Murray* (ed. Pearce, B L) due to be published by the Palgrave Society; together with letters from the poet and his brothers.

3 Cf. Palgrave (F T): *Selected Poems*; edited with an introduction by Pearce, B L. Brentham Press, 1985. 17

4 Palgrave, G F: Francis Turner Palgrave ..., 1899; reprint (USA), 1971 (cf the poem "Absence")

5 Courtesy of John Murray, publisher, and Virginia Murray, archivist; the Master and Fellows of Trinity College, Cambridge; *Correspondence of Arthur Hugh Clough*, edited F Mulhauser. Oxford, 1987 (2 vols.); *The Palgraves to John Murray*, letters; edited Pearce, B L. Palgrave Society (in the press).

6 Cf. Ref.3, and Pearce, B L: *The Fashioned Reed*, BOTLHS, 1992, 31-37

7 For the full facts see Ref.3, 9-11

8 The 1926 edition (edited R Brimley Johnson), 139-140

9 Cf. Appendix I or the paper it is based on: Pearce, B L: Glow and afterglow: the criteria and influence of the "Golden Treasury", *Acumen* (24) January 1996, 23-26

10 Cf. the hymn and G Horder's comment on its expression of "the difficulty and longing of our day for faith" in Ref.3, 27 & 63. It thus refers back to the central problems discussed in connection with Clough and Arnold.

11 Cf. Ref.3, 26-27, 63

12 Cf. Ref.3, 51-2

13 Cf. the chalk drawing of him by S Laurence 1872, frontispiece of Ref.3, courtesy of National Portrait Gallery.

14 Cf. Ref.9 and the Arnold study above, where he is cited.

15 Cf. *Poetry for Children* Third Book; ed. E A Helps, Bell, 1884. (Contains "Love's Language" and "Margaret Wilson")

16 Cf. Pearce, B L: Palgrave and "The Visions of England", Ore (33), 1985, 9-13

17 Part quoted in Pearce, B L: *Hail to the Queen: Verses for Queen Victoria's Jubilee, 1887* (A4 pamphlet) Magwood/Brentham, 1987, 9-11; cf. also Pearce, B L: "Jubilee Verses". Jnl Soc. of Arts CXXXV (5372) July 1987, 573-4

18 Cf. Ref.3, 60-61, for all seven verses.

19 - and on Shairp's *On Poetic Interpretation of Nature*, 1887, in my opinion

20 Cf. Ref.9

21 Based on a lecture given at the National Portrait Gallery on 24th October, 1990, on the anniversary of his death, and on the publications cited.

22 See also Appendix I.

9. THE CATHOLICS

The preceding poets were all, nominally at least, Anglicans, whatever their doubts or anxieties; Palgrave had Tractarian leanings and admired Newman, it is true. The next poets to be discussed were or, more accurately, became Catholics. Thus they have common ground with the older Newman who, as it happens, showed characteristic consideration to Hopkins at a critical moment in the latter's career. All three started outside the Catholic fold and Patmore's first wife was a Congregational minister's daughter. Newman's own poetry has its distinction. Who would not be proud to have created the text that inspired Elgar to compose his masterpiece *The Dream of Gerontius*, whilst the writer cannot be the sole Free Churchman to have sung "Lead kindly light" ... "o'er crag and torrent, till/ the night is gone" with emotion? As his novels; *Apologia pro vita sua*, and *The Idea of a University*[1], show in their different ways, Newman was a considerable literary artist, as well as a great theologian and devotional spirit, and had he wished could easily have enlarged his creative oeuvre. But his priority was to his spiritual fervour and it is that spirit, plainly, which informs and gives the particular distinctive quality to his work: one cannot isolate the concepts, and to lose the devotion, in such a case as his, would be to lose the essence of his power.

It is Hopkins who knew Newman, but Patmore, the older of the three poets, who forms a personal link between them. Toward the end of his life he came to know both Hopkins and Meynell and, proud man as he was, to admire them both. Their poetry, however, is quite dissimilar. Patmore's, at first all too accessible, became obscure and difficult; Hopkins', difficult too, and needing "work" if he is to be fully appreciated, rewards us by proving the most intense and fervent *feeler and* consummate poetic *artist* of his era (possibly since the Romantics) in the way he combines spiritual and human emotion so that we can't see the weld or stitch, and pens it in as though the force of its lava can only be constrained by steel bands - and does this with the most exquisite refinement of sensibility. But his will always be a personal appeal, possibly, since it concerns the individual, God-oriented spirit. Alice Meynell is quieter, less ambitious ostensibly, but not necessarily all that less intense, and hers is a sensitivity not so very distinct from that of Virginia Woolf's, on occasion. Fastidious in her discrimination and restraint, she rewards the discriminating reader. A fourth poet, Francis Thompson, has been subsumed under her essay, rather than given separate treatment, partly because he was befriended by Alice and William Meynell, partly because his poetry seems too diffuse, ultimately, and to lack a centre. He has some fine things that continue to hold their own, "In No Strange Lane", "To a Daisy" or "The Hound of Heaven", and a poem or two to Alice; the magnificent prose of his essay on Shelley and his ode on

Victoria's 1897 Jubilee; a longer list than what endures of Patmore's, perhaps. But in Patmore there is an aspiration and intention, an elevation and proliferation of ideas that, magnificent failure as he may be, gives him the greater stature. He is a would-be synthesiser of earth and heaven and no mean seer, as Sargent contrives to bring out in his striking N.P.G portrait.

Lionel Johnson's work[2] is craftsmanly, and often compact with fervour, as in the sonnet "Bagley Wood" or the Marvellian "Statue of King Charles", or some of his poems on Winchester; but nowhere more so than in "The Dark Angel" or "Mystic and Cavalier" ("Go from me: I am one of those who fall"), where he is tragically, powerfully himself. His study "The Art of Thomas Hardy" (on the fiction) is a fine book, and he knew Yeats who numbers him amongst the "tragic generation" of the 'nineties.

Chesterton, Belloc, Baring, subjects brought together in James Gunn's Conversation Piece[3], produced good poems and are sympathetic figures but the weight of their legacy is in their prose. It is highly readable prose, too, competent, thoughtful and appealing. Chesterton, who started as a Unitarian, lived to tell the tales of *Father Brown*, psychologically so compelling, and *The Man who was Thursday*, a paradoxical tour de force. Baring's amusing historical reconstructions await re-discovery.[4] Evidence abundant there is, here, of Catholic encouragement of art and literature during the period. The Unitarians have their Mrs Gaskell; the Independents William Hale White ("Mark Rutherford"), but for most Nonconformists the vehicle of literary ambition was the hymn. Amongst this flourishing company of Catholic practitioners, Patmore, Hopkins and Meynell, for their different reasons, stand out.

Notes
1 Cf. Pearce, B L: "The Idea of Newman and the Useful Arts" *Jrnl. RSA CXXXVIII* (5412), November 1990, 847-849
2 Cf. *The Complete Poems of Lionel Johnson*, edited Iain Fletcher, 1953
3 Cf. The picture in the National Portrait Gallery on which the author lectured, 15.3.1994
4 Cf. *Maurice Baring Restored*; edited Paul Horgen, 1970

10. PATMORE

"The greatest poet of the nineteenth century", said Alice Meynell of Coventry Patmore (1823-1896), twenty-five years after he had died, yet he finds but few readers in our day. Patmore made his mark as the poet of married love, who found the Divine love mirrored in the human. He married three times, on the first occasion when he was twenty-four, from which point his life can be divided into three distinct phases, the aptness of which is poetic in itself.

First Marriage: 15 years till his wife dies: the lyrical poetry: popularity: wife Congregational: great happiness;

Second Marriage: 15 year till his wife dies: the esoteric odes: wife Catholic: he becomes a Catholic: wife's ill-health requires governess: popularity starts to wane;

Third Marriage: to governess: 15 years till his death: the prose reflections: finds inspiration in a younger woman, herself a writer.

Coventry Kersey Dighton Patmore was born at Woodford, Essex, on 23rd July 1823. His first name stems from his godmother, the Hon. Mrs Coventry. His father, Peter George Patmore, a friend of Hazlitt and Lamb, incurred opprobrium through being a second at a duel at which his principal was killed, and by Hazlitt's injudicious publication of letters to him, rehearsing Hazlitt's regard for his landlady's daughter. He speculated in railway shares to unhappy effect and had to flee the country, leaving his family in straightened circumstances, and published a volume of memoirs which provoked further criticism. His library was available to his son, however, and he encouraged the publication of Coventry's first book of poetry. His mother, Eliza Robertson, a Scotswoman, appears to have influenced his upbringing less than his grandmother, herself a daughter of the German painter Baekermann. She gave him warmth and affection and probably his latent artistic gift, evident at the age of 14 when in 1838 he was awarded a silver palette by the Society of Arts for a pencil copy of an animal drawing. The following year he spent six months at a school in France, and was enamoured of a Miss Gore. It was at this time that he wrote his first poems and first proposed to himself, such is the idealism of youth, the subjects of his later work. When later he came across a portrait that resembled her he set it on the wall behind shutters and spoke of it as portraying the "first angel", referring to the title of his most popular book. He returned to England; dabbled in science; thought about holy orders, but was deterred by scruples and his father's inability to pay for a university education. He remained of a religious mind, however, and did not emulate his father in his freethinking.

In 1844 he published *Poems*. "The Tale of Poor Maud", one of its four narratives, led to Millais' *The Woodman's Daughter* exhibited at the Royal Academy in 1851. This was one of Millais' first essays in contemporary life. His father's financial failure made it imperative for Patmore to earn a living and in 1846 Monkton Milnes (later Lord Houghton) secured him a post in the printed book department of the British Museum. The post appears to have been congenial and his work competent. It is incidental that he may have had a hand in his benefactor's *Life of Keats* (1848) though, if so, it was as one of the earliest of ghost-writers. In 1847 he married Emily Augusta Andrews, daughter of a Congregational minister; a young woman of uncommon charm and common sense, with her own spiritual and literary gifts. Patmore was 23, she a year younger. He proposed to her on Hampstead Heath; they were married in Hampstead Church, and afterwards lived in the Highgate/Hampstead area and Bloomsbury. Millais painted her portrait, whilst Browning wrote the poem "A Face" in her honour:

If one could have that little head of hers
Painted upon a background of pale gold ...

So commenced 15 years of great happiness, productive not only of three sons and three daughters but the most part of his traditional-style lyric poetry. In *Tamerton Church Tower & other poems* (1853;54):

The clouds, uneven, black and near,
And ragged at the marge ...

we find an artistic sensitivity, and observation of nature akin to Tennyson's and Virginia Woolf's or, indeed to that of his future co-religionists Hopkins and Alice Meynell; an attempt at "scientific" exactitude not altogether alien to Constable's wish to be regarded as a natural historian.[1-3] He and his wife's happiness must have contributed greatly to his best-known poem *The Angel in the House* (1853-1866), which enjoyed such popularity at the time of its publication despite its sometimes too obvious and flaccid quatrains, the rhyming jingle of which, combined with a lively narrative, no doubt contributed to its success. It is an ambitious (readable as well as edifying) tribute to courtship and married love, better, as we might, expect on courtship. It is significant that so many tales conclude ..."and they lived happily ever after," for though happiness may be a fact it is less exciting to read about than the agitation and suspense that precedes it. *The Betrothals* appeared in 1854; *Espousals* in 1856; *Faithful for Ever* in 1860 and the graver *The Victories of Love* in 1863. There is charm:

Breakfast enjoy'd, 'mid hush of boughs
And perfumes thro' the windows blown ...

feeling for mood, and refreshing directness in the courtship:

> The moods of love are like the wind,
> And none knows whence or why they rise:
> I ne'er before felt heart and mind
> So much affected through mine eyes.
> How cognate with the flatter'd air,
> How form'd for earth's familiar zone,
> She moved; how feeling and how fair
> For others' pleasure and her own ... ("Sarum Plain")

The proclaimed subject of *domestic* love, so much more difficult admittedly, he perhaps manages here:

> Why, having won her, do I woo?
> Because her spirit's vestal grace
> Provokes me always to pursue,
> But, spirit-like, eludes embrace;
> Because her womanhood is such
> That, as on court-days subjects kiss
> The Queen's hand, yet so near a touch
> Affirms no mean familiarness ... ("The Married Lover")

It is true this relates more to an early domesticity than the welded unity of the years in which the prized condition may include indistinguishable elements of affection, support, accommodation and companionship; in which, indeed, "familiarness" can be its greatest reward. Even in these, early, comparatively-lighthearted poems, however, we find his great theme, his constant pre-occupation: the mirroring of Divine love in the human, and the intermingling of the two. It has something of Plato and the Song of Songs; something of Keats' "finer tone" and Yeats': "For things below are copies, as the great Smaraggdine Tablet says." It has more than a little of Blake and Swedenborg in it. In "Heaven and Earth" he makes his position clear:

> How long shall men deny the flower
> Because its roots are in the earth
> ... fools shall feel like fools to find
> (Too late inform'd) that angels' mirth
> Is one in cause, and mode, and kind
> With that which they profaned on earth.

as throughout *The Angel in the House*, with all honesty, I think, if with unconscious self-deception, and intrinsic idealism:

> I loved her in the name of God,
> And for the ray she was of Him;
> I ought to admire much more, not less;
> Her beauty was a godly grace;
> The mystery of loveliness
> Which made an altar of her face ...

or:

Him loved I most
But her I loved most sensibly.

There is an intriguing, ambiguous dedication to the edition of 1885: "This poem is inscribed to the memory of her by whom and for whom I became a poet." Emily assisted him with the editing of his *Children's Garland* anthology of 1862, and was herself author of one or two small ("useful") books under the pseudonym of "Mrs Motherly". He sought to augment his income by writing for the reviews, though he found it uncongenial since, as the DNB puts it, "he could take no vital interest in anyone's ideas but his own." Yet this combative, rancorous, egoistic, susceptible, tender riddle of a man - who could not see others' great things or his own follies - pursued his ideals (and devotions) to the end, and was the friend of such equally distinct personalities as Carlyle, Browning, Tennyson, Ruskin and the Pre-Raphaelites, Hopkins, Gosse and Alice Meynell, in all of whom we see aspiration or idealism as a common (if characteristically Victorian) feature. At one time, he was particularly close to the Pre-Raphaelites. He knew Rossetti and contributed to"The Germ". He was friendly with Holman Hunt. It was he who, at Millais' request, won Ruskin to their championship at a critical juncture. In contrast to them, however, he did write largely about his own time, and was concerned with it; hence his promotion of the volunteer movement, after Louis Napoleon's coup-d'etat in December 1851. Rarely as his work approaches Browning or Tennyson's best, they with Ruskin and Carlyle, were amongst those who praised it. Characteristic of those happier touches to which they may have responded is a poem like "The Rosy Bosom's Hours" in which he tells of two days of radiant happiness, his hopes of a third and his disappointment when "As at dusk (they) reached Penzance,/ A drizzling rain set in,"[4] or his picture of a tree "... With bitter ivy bound; / Terraced with funguses unsound;/ Deformed with many a boss/ And closed scar, o'er cushioned deep with moss ...",[5] with its dense luxuriant decay, akin to passages in Rossetti or Tennyson's "Mariana", in his (Patmore's) later manner.

Alas, Emily died of consumption on 4th July 1862, and their productive honeymoon of a marriage was brought to a tragic end. Maria Jackson (née Pattle) took his children into her own home and looked after them until a more permanent solution could be found. Patmore's description of Maria as "the dearest friend I had"[6] should be read in the context he wrote it, in a letter of condolence on her death; even so, it is a remarkable testament. He missed Emily greatly and in the hope of restoring his spirits visited Rome in 1864. Dropping his chauvinist critiques of French cuisine, like many a cantankerous northerner before him he mellowed wonderfully once he encountered the transforming geniality of Italy's warmth and light, and wrote:

... worth a thousand mile journey ... a lovely, little faint-peach-coloured town crowded itself together, like a flock of sheep when the dog barks round it ... the mist ... the sides of mountains so beautifully chasmed, chiselled and dotted ... with olives and oranges ... and the whole bathed in a spacious gulf of delicate air, burthened at intervals with drifting coils of golden and swiftly dissolving clouds ...[7]

No wonder Carlyle had written to him:

... whether it had not been better that a man of your powers had trained himself to *prose* as exquisitely as you have to verse, and stood by the rigorous fact ... instead of floating, in this light, beautiful way ... above it ... now take some more robust class of subjects, and close the *Troubadour* Enterprise ...[8]

Carlyle may have been right, though the result might not have been the imitation of himself he perhaps had in view.

In Rome he met Marianne Caroline Byles (generally known as Mary), a little over forty (so of a similar age to himself), daughter of a landowner, a Catholic, pious and reserved - said to have resembled Emily in appearance. She had contemplated entering the convent, having at one time been close to Henry (subsequently Cardinal) Manning, before he converted to Rome. It was Manning, indeed, who married them at Mary of the Angels, Bayswater, in 1865. Patmore converted to Catholicism himself - a change that Emily had foreseen as likely - and so entered his second main creative period, that of the difficult, diffuse, jerky paragraphs of *The Unknown Eros*, in which so many jewels are embedded. He had an outer life as well as an inner, however; gave up his job at the British Museum, for Mary was a woman of substance, and bought an estate of 400 acres near Uckfield, Sussex, which he named Heron's Ghyll. Later he was to dispose of it and settle at The Mansion, Hastings, a fine house which (in parallel with the case of Dickens) had taken his fancy as a child. In 1886 he published *How I Managed and Improved my Estate* and gave a copy of the pamphlet to Gerard Manley Hopkins who first overlooked that he had received it and then replied that the work would have been very useful to him had he had an estate.[9]

The *Odes* of this second phase saw a preliminary appearance in 1868, when he circulated nine of them for the private attention of his literary friends.[10] Involved in their style and thought, and rarely succinct, it is not difficult to see why the response was daunting. The most positive response came from Ruskin, and that was praise faint indeed: "It is needful to thank you for the book you sent me ... I recognise the nobleness of the last ("1867") ... the first ("Prophets who cannot sing") shall help me as it may ..." Patmore burnt most of his remaining copies, his daughter Emily saving a few from the flames. Writing much later, he explains his method thus:

Nearly all English metres owe their existence as metres to "catalexis" or pause, for the time of one or more feet, and, as a rule, the position and amount of catalexis are fixed. But the verse in which this volume is written is catalectic par excellence, employing the pause (as it does the rhyme) with freedom only limited by the exigencies of poetic passion. ... The licence to rhyme at indefinite intervals is counterbalanced, in the writing of all poets who have employed this metre successfully, by unusual frequency in the recurrence of the same rhyme.[11]

The odes were not popular, as *The Angel in the House* had been, nor much understood by his peers. The problem is partly the elusive nature of the thought since a similar method works for W E Henley's *London Voluntaries*, though it is true Henley is not wrestling with spiritual profundities.[12] Patmore's mysticism may be of importance for its own sake, ultimately, rather than for its intrinsic poetic merit, but it is a pity that it is a mysticism out of print. In *The Unknown Eros & other odes* of 1877, as in the (trial) nine, he continues to inter-relate human love and the Divine with high-minded ardour, producing many fine passages. There are poems that have a clear narrative engagement, such as "Departure" on Emily's death,[13] which it seems an intrusion to quote, or the much anthologised "The Toys"[14], with its sympathetic detail ("He had put, within his reach,/ A box of counters and a red-vein'd stone ...") though it is difficult to deny Alice Meynell's opinion that it has less essential poetry in it than almost any other of the odes. The boy was his son Milnes, whose difficult early start at sea was embodied by Conrad in his novel *Chance*, not one of his absolute masterpieces and therefore the book that first endeared him to a wider public. Conrad portrays the poet as an arrogant sentimentalist, whose rapport was not of the best. There is *some* point in the caricature, but in key aspects it is unfounded. Patmore was more sensual than sentimental, and would never have seen virtue in a non-consummated marriage, a point on which the plot turns. He was a well-intentioned, moral man, with a genuine piety, even humility, if we may take this for counterpoise:

No praise to me!
My joy was to be nothing but the glass
Through which the general boon of heaven should pass,
To focus upon thee ...
Blind fumblers that we be
About the portals of felicity! ... ("Semele")

Here we come nearer the key moods of the odes. Patmore is amongst the handful of poets who could write, as he does in "To the Body" of a love "Quick, tender, virginal and unprofaned," or in "Deliciae Sapientiae de Amore":

Ye to whom generous love, by any name, is dear.
Love makes the life to be ...
And who Him love, in potence great or small,
Are, one and all,
Heirs ...

Or, earlier in the poem:

The magnet calls the steel.
Answers the iron to the magnet's breath,
What do they feel
But death!
The clouds of summer kiss in flame and rain,
And are not found again;

> But the heavens themselves eternal are with fire
> Of unapproach'd desire,
> By the aching heart of Love, which cannot rest,
> In blissfullest pathos so indeed possess'd ...

Unmistakeable in its mystical merging of two spheres is this from "Sponsa Dei":

> What if this Lady by thy Soul, and He
> Who claims to enjoy her sacred beauty be
> Not Thou, but God; and thy sick fire
> A female vanity ...

But equally telling are phrases in the less-cited poem "The Child's Purchase", with its "Ora pro me!" refrain which helps tie it together:

> The extreme of God's creative energy;
> Sunshiny Peak of human personality;
> The world's sad aspiration's one Success ...
> His Infinite reposed in thy finite ...
> To fire my verse with thy shy fame ...

It is a question of the greatest tenderness allied with the greatest power (and is that not Christ-like?); of a love which energises both itself and the one by whom it is inspired, and which gives life to the attributes it sees or wishes to discover.[15] In our lightest love the flame of the holiest is to be perceived, Patmore says.

Patmore's second wife was much engaged in prayer and meditation; her health was poor, and in 1880 she died. For some time the ordering of the household had devolved upon the governess, Harriet Robson, and in 1881 she became Patmore's third wife.[16] She had exercised discretion during the second marriage and was to do so in her own, as when Patmore became friendly with Alice Meynell, and she continued to do her duty in rolling his cigarettes. In 1882 his daughter Emily died and in 1883, Henry, his youngest son by his first wife, died of pleurisy. Some of Henry's poems are included in the 1886 collection of Patmore's poetry. It was an edition that owed something to the careful emendations of none other than Gerard Manley Hopkins; Patmore had met him on a visit to Stoneyhurst on 29th July 1883. It says much for both men that the stubborn, irascible veteran was to take his suggestions in good part; enter into prolonged correspondence, and remain on good terms with the younger poet who went in for such profound and avant-garde technicalities.[17] It has to do with their powerful (though variant) sensuality; their common religion, and their common fervour in relating both to their art, though Patmore must have found him congenial in general and respected his intelligence.[18] There is some interest in the fact that Hopkins, writing to Patmore of his son Henry, takes a line very similar to Carlyle's:

> I shd. say he had, and would have found himself to have, a command of prose style by which he could have achieved more even than by that of poetry. The finest prose style in, in English,

at least, rarer, I would say, than the finest poetical.[19]

Patmore's third "phase" did, indeed, see him concentrating on prose, though we shall see that in one point at least, Hopkins' advice was less happy. The prose consists of two kinds: collections of his essays and articles on literature and art, and reflections and aphorisms on themes such as the interaction and parallelism of Divine and human love which had actuated and absorbed him from the first. *Principle in Art* (1889) is of the first order; *Religio Poetae* (1893)[20] inclines to the second, and *The Rod, the Root and the Flower* (1895) inclines more closely still. There should have been a fourth book, *Sponsa Dei*, intimate reflections, "polished and modulated to the highest degree of perfection" (Gosse) on which he had been working for years, in which his thoughts on human and Divine love were most fully articulated. It concerned the "relation of the soul to Christ as his betrothed wife"; and "interpretation of the love between the soul and God by an analogy of the love between a woman and a man ... a transcendental treatise on Divine desire seen through the veil of human desire" (Gosse). In this instance Hopkins was an unfortunate choice for adviser, seeing that he was a priest and neither a married man himself or one who had been a lover of women. His advice was against publication, seeing it as of too intimate and dangerous a character. He did suggest obtaining the opinion of Dr Rouse whose advice also came down (if mildly) on the side of non-publication. So "on Xmas Day" Patmore burnt the book, "without reserve of a single paragraph."[21] So it went the same way as Byron's memoirs or (in effect) the conclusion of Morris's *Novel on Blue Paper*, though there may be something of its substance in *The Rod, the Root, and the Flower*. It is a pity he could not have put it to one side, or entrusted it to a lawyer's vault. Hopkins had the grace to regret his advice not having been couched more provisionally, but it was too late.[22] In a letter to Bridges of 12th August 1889, Hopkins having died in June, Patmore writes:

> The authority of his goodness was so great with me that I threw the MS of a little book ... into the fire ... (it) had been the work of ten years ... but his doubt was final with me.

It was late in his life that he met his fellow Catholic journalist and poet, Alice Meynell (née Thompson, born 1847) with whom he was to enjoy an honourable, energising and very tender friendship, though it was too late to fructify in any work of substance. E J Oliver writes:

> Her effect on Patmore was intoxicating. She really extended the range of his perceptions, which came to him chiefly through women, because she was a woman he had never met before, indeed a woman who had never existed before. What Gosse did in making his work known to the younger generation, she did in making the younger generation known to him.[23]

She must have extended his creative life a little, if not to the extent that Kamila Stosslova did for Janacek, and certainly gave him immense happiness, if mixed with the inevitable agitation. She may have influenced him, unconsciously, in *The Rod, the Root, and the Flower* and, if so, more valuably than in the pieces he wrote in her honour: "A rustle on the staircase/Gives the heart gay warning", or:

Her body, too, is so like her -
Sharp honey assuaged with milk,
Straight as a stalk of lavender,
Soft as a rope of silk.[24]

His wry jealousy of George Meredith's place in her feelings, or Francis Thompson's place at her table; his mien when denied the chance of a word with her, is easily comprehensible. Alice's purity of spirit, and innate sensitivity and tact, enabled her to handle his affection without discredit to either party, or unhappiness in the family to which she gave devoted care. She edited an anthology of his work, *The Poetry of Pathos and Delight*, an enterprise which, as the DNB says, she must have "undertaken with all her heart." He will have been one she had in mind when in later life she wrote of her "failure of love to those that loved me."

So we have the three main phases of his mature career: the lyric, the esoteric odes, and the reflective, emotive prose. In 1891 he moved to Lymington, in Hampshire, when a change of ownership of his Hastings home compelled a move. It was Edmund Gosse who urged Patmore to sit for his portrait to Sargent in summer 1894, resulting in the masterly vibrant oil now in the National Portrait Gallery. Its kit-kat scale emphasises the lean body, compact with nervous energy; the immense sense of emotional and visionary force, a virility of soul, in the scragged features and carcase of an ageing man. The gaze is steady, the combative fist clenched at the hip. Accepted amongst his contemporaries as a faithful likeness, if he had been shown smoking the effect would have been complete: "fearfully like" wrote Patmore himself. Sargent is said to have engaged him in political conversation in order to promote indignation and Gosse insisted that Patmore was "not always thus ragged and vulturine, not always such a miraculous portent of gnarled mandible and shaken plumage," while Champneys, his early biographer, thought it emphasised the outward "truculent" character at the expense of the "seer." The "seer", in a more reflective, softer visionary mood, is perhaps better caught in a sketch Sargent did during the same sittings, to be used for a portrait of Ezekiel in a scheme of mural decoration for the Boston (USA) public library.

On 26th November 1896 Patmore died of pneumonia, his resting place at Lymington being marked by an obelisk. In the preface to the 1885 edition of his poems he had written:

I have written little, but it is all my best. I have never spoken when I had nothing to say, nor spared time or labour to make my words true. I have respected posterity; and, should there be a posterity which cares for letters, I dare to hope that it will respect me. [25,26]

Notes

1 *The Poems of Coventry Patmore*, ed. Page, F. Oxford, 1949

2 The passage is to be found in Grigson, G. *The Faber Book of Poems and Places*, 1980, 89-92.

3 Two verses are quoted in Pearce, B.L. "Coventry Patmore (1823-1896)" *Journal RSA CXLIV* (5467) March 1996, 69-71, where his artistic gift and receipt of the Society's award are discussed.

4 *Pall Mall Gazette*, 6 July 1876; Ricks, C., ed. *The New Oxford Book of Victorian Verse*, O.U.P., 1987, 322-324

5 "Arbor Vitae", Ricks, 325-6

6 Hill, B. *Julia Margaret Cameron*. P. Owen, 1973, 158-9

7 Oliver, E.J. *Coventry Patmore*, 1956, 82-3

8 Oliver, 32

9 Hopkins, G.M. *Further Letters of Hopkins* (letters to Coventry Patmore *et al*); edited by C C Abbott, Oxford 1938 (1956 rev. & enl.). Cf. letters of Nov 7, 1886 and Jan 20, 1887.

10 *Odes* (1868); edited with a bibliography by John Merrell. Tamerton Press facsimile, n.d. (c1960's?) Important not least for JM's annotations to the checklist, including the emendation of at least one date.

11 Preface to the 3rd edition of *The Unknown Eros and other odes*, Bell, 1890

12 But at least, in the method, Patmore could claim to be a pioneer. It is interesting that his subsequent friend Hopkins should have been the one, quite independently, to develop the sprung rhythm idea. See also Pearce, B.L. "The London Voluntaries" (of W E Henley) *Ore* (28), 1982, 13-19

13 Oliver, 75-6 (there is a certain selfishness here, as so often in grief)

14 Ricks, 324-5

15 Cf. Pearce, B.L. "In this sparked/ polarit-/y is the/ force that makes/ flesh and breaks/ open tombs". "Gift Header". *Coeli et Terra*, Chicago, 1993, 18-20 or "the way/ she plumed in empathy" "Collared" in "City Whiskers" Stride, 1996, 108

16 Something of Hardy's relationship with *his* second wife, Florence Dugdale, can be seen here.

17 Patmore seems to have been more sympathetic than Bridges, in some respects.

18 And goodness. Cf. Ref. 9, Patmore's letter to Bridges, 12th August 1889.

19 Cf. Ref. 9. GMH writing from Stoneyhurst, 23rd November 1883.

20 The title essay to *Religio Poetae*; "Love and Poetry" and "Dieu et ma Dame" exemplify the second type, e.g. (from "Dieu et ma Dame"): "each (the man and the woman) being equally, though not alike, a manifestation of the Divine to the other."

21 See Ref. 9, letter of Feb 10th 1888.

22 See Ref. 9, letter of May 6th 1888.

23 See Ref. 7, 179

24 *Alice Meynell's Poetry and Prose*; ed. V Sackville-West, Cape, 1947, 9.32

25 Based on a lecture given at the National Portrait Gallery on 15th June 1994

26 See also Burdett, O. *The Idea of Coventry Patmore*, Oxford, 1921; and Page, F. *Patmore: a study in poetry*, Oxford, 1933

11. HOPKINS

Gerard Manley Hopkins (1844-1889), poet, Jesuit priest, acute observer of Nature, was born at 87 The Grove, Stratford, London E15, on the 28th July 1844. The house was destroyed by a bomb in 1941 and the busy road system about its site scarcely fits with this sensitive aesthete, scholar and tutor of devotional temper, sensuous to the extreme yet disciplined to the hilt. He might easily have been a painter or a musician in other circumstances. His poetry is distinguished by the utmost feeling (both tactile and devotional in origin) ordered by intensest exercise of an outstanding intellect and will. It would burst its side with rapture, grief and invention were it not subject to such compelling control, as it demonstrates variety (and restraint) of fervour par excellence. It celebrates the natural word; is sometimes rapturous with gladness. It contains dark spiritual questioning; anguish close to despair, yet always, if barely, triumphs over it. Its language is terse, exuberant, original, complex, foreshortened by turns; its artefacts tight-hammered vessels of meaning and sound, the very tautness of which increases their power. Take the difference in mood and range of "Pied Beauty" or "The Windhover", on one hand, and "The Wreck of the Deutschland" or one of the late "terrible" sonnets on the other; yet in each mood, and in large compass or small, we can find his powers at their best. Fifty pages of Hopkins are as great a legacy - such is their intensity and artistry - and have as great a resonance in their modest volume, as the whole oeuvre of many of his peers, though it is true that a reader may find him "difficult" initially; need to "work" at him, and perhaps to be on a similar "wavelength." It is not because his work was not put before the literary world till some thirty years after his death that he speaks to so many today, whilst the voices of several famous contemporaries fade, but because of his freshness and honesty, his ongoing relevance to the individual heart and soul, and his control, seen best in his poetry but also to be traced in his notebooks, sketchbooks and letters. Did his priesthood advance or retard his development? It was responsible for the loss of seven years work, which in any life, especially a short one, is sad. Yet in banking the Muse and narrowing its stream, his vocation doubtless increased the force of its flow, the sensuous/ priestly-conscience tension being at its source. One thing is sure. Priest and poet were bound up together; they were one and the same person, and we cannot separate them. Each helps to define what the other is. Christian impulse and conscience is central to Hopkins' life *and* work; inherent in every thought, and comes out in every syllable.

His father, Manley Hopkins, was a marine insurer, with his own London firm. He was also Consul-General for Hawaii in London, and himself published three books of poetry. His mother Kate (Catherine Simm Smith) was the daughter of a London doctor. It is ironic that she lived until 1920, when she was nearly 100 and that seven siblings lived past the First World War, three of them surviving till 1945, 1946 and 1952, respectively, and seeing the end of the Second, yet their brother, the "marvellous boy" died in 1889, just before his 45th birthday - and yet it is he who most "lives" today. An unmarried aunt, Eleanor, lived with the family and encouraged the children in art, music and archaeology.[1] Hence the sketching talent of Gerard and others; the training his observation must have had, and the musical talent of his sister Grace. His brother Lionel shared his linguistic gifts; was a scholar of Chinese language, and the last survivor, dying in 1952, some 63 years after the poet, somehow linking him physically with a later world.

In 1852 the family moved to Oakhill House, Hampstead, where it was to remain for 34 years.[2] Residence in Hampstead raises curious parallels. There is Keats' fresh zest, great gifts and early death; the similarity in mood of Coleridge's and Hopkins' late sonnets; the effect of Hampstead Heath on Housman; with the shared gusto of the out-of-doors and of deep-felt male friendship; the quick inspiration followed by hard labour in completing a poem; the fact that they both became Professors of Classics. For two years Hopkins went to a day school in Hampstead; in September 1854, at the age of ten, he entered Highgate School[3] where he was to stay for eight years. He started as a day boy but ended as a boarder at Elgin House. His headmaster was the Revd. Dr Dyne who struck Gerard with his riding whip, deprived him of his room, sent him to bed at nine, ordered him to work only in the schoolroom and threatened him with expulsion. It can only be that it is in poets and similar, reflective spirits, inoffensive and defenceless as they may appear, that authority of the parade ground sort[4] discerns the inner spirit of resistance glowing most keenly: certain it is that in the upbringing of Victorian and Edwardian writers we hear much of such indefensible regimens. It beggers thought why Dyne singled out Hopkins, gentle and happy to study. Like Swinburne, however, his moral and physical courage, and independence of spirit, defied his frail build. The splendid thing is that his early enthusiasms did not change. When he was at Stoneyhurst, in his late thirties, a lay brother described him as "a strange young man, crouching down ... to stare at some wet sand." At Highgate, despite or because of what he experienced under Dyne, he won prizes for classics, a gold medal for Latin verse, an exhibition to Balliol and a prize for his poem "The Escorial". It was there, too, that he wrote "A Vision of the Mermaids" and "Winter with the Gulf Stream", the latter being published when he was eighteen, almost the only poem to be published in his lifetime. Keats and the Pre-Raphaelites were early influences. The poet R W Dixon spent a few months teaching at the school and described Hopkins then as "a pale young boy, very light and active, with a very meditative and intellectual face." He did a fair amount of sketching at Highgate, and left with a love of the Classics which he always retained.

In April 1863 he went up to Balliol, following in the footsteps of the "Scholars" we have discussed, Arnold, Palgrave and Clough. The college was at the height of its scholarly and intellectual activity and in 1866 Hopkins was to get a first in "Greats" - honours in Greek, Latin, philosophy and ancient history. Benjamin Jowett was not yet Master of Balliol but a formidable Fellow. He aimed at the Socratic ideal; to seek truth by question and answer; not to impart his own ideas but to encourage his students to use their own minds. It was this intellectual "purity" which impressed Hopkins. The idealist philosopher T H Green was also an influence. Moral earnestness, scholarship, and linguistic ability were all qualities to which he particularly responded. Hopkins was happy at Oxford, and socially and intellectually active. He had friends; walked, swam, took pleasure in boating. There are parallels with Clough; with Brooke's enjoyment of swimming at Cambridge; with Swinburne's love of the sea and of swimming. Swinburne was a poet he admired, though he recognised that his own aims were different. The Pre-Raphaelite painters, and Ruskin, also exerted an influence especially the latter's emphasis on getting at the truth of Nature. In 1865 he was reading Arnold, and heard him lecture. His friends included William Addis, sometime Freechurchman, Catholic priest, Presbyterian minister, Unitarian, and Anglican priest; Alexander Baillie, barrister and recipient of many letters, and Robert Bridges, the future laureate, who received so many of the poet's letters and (with so scant real sympathy or comprehension) his slim poetic corpus as it accumulated, and published it, after so long a delay, with a harsh preface, in 1918. Yet friends they were, from their meeting in Oxford, born in the same year. By 1865 Hopkins was going through a period of intense religious tension and self-examination, and had started to go to the Tractarians E B Puscy and H P Liddon for confession. There is something of Housman's feeling for Moses Jackson in Hopkins' 1865 sonnet line: "Where art thou friend, whom I shall never see." Hopkins had just met the 17-year old Digby Dolben, himself a poet, who died by drowning in 1867, and there may be relevance in the better known lines in the late sonnet: "cries like dead letters sent/ To dearest him that lives alas! away."[5] One is constantly struck by his ability to combine emotion and aesthetic sensibility with the keenest moral asceticism, devotion to the person of Jesus, intellectual rigour and steely self-discipline. It is the polarity of these clements, and their welding together by mind and will - given that he was equipped with exceptional powers - that is the key to his life and art. High moral tone was much in evidence in Victorian Oxford, whether modelled on Dr Arnold's rugged kind, Kingsley's militant kind, Jowett's intellectual enquiry, Newman's intellectual and devotional search for authority, or Keble's and Pusey's devotional purity. But in few men do we see such fusion of Paterian aestheticism and Newman-like devotion and intellectual control as in Gerard Manley Hopkins, or see it to have creative issue of such a high order. Pater, Fellow of Brasenose, author of *The Renaissance* and *Marius the Epicurean*, was actually Hopkins' tutor in the Easter term of 1866, and they remained in sympathy though differing in their beliefs. "To burn always with his hard, gemlike flame, to maintain this ecstasy, is success in life", wrote Pater at the end of *The Renaissance*. "Hard, gemlike" ... is that not how we might describe Hopkins' best work? It is understandable that Hopkins should warm to that intense aesthetic appreciation, yet feel the need to temper it with his religious ascetic sense and, indeed, to distance himself from it; yet it is the tension between these elements which (whatever pain or difficulty it brought to him) gives his work its quivering life. Take "Hurrahing in Harvest" (Penguin 15) or the kingfisher poem (Penguin 34). "What I do is me: for that I came ... (to act) in God's eye ...", he writes in the latter poem.

He was increasingly exercised as to whether he should remain in the Church of England. The question of authority haunted him as it had Newman, and like Newman he turned to Rome. It was to Newman personally that he turned in September 1866 and the future Cardinal treated him with characteristic consideration. It was Newman who received him into the Catholic Church on 21st October 1866. It was Newman who encouraged him to remain at Oxford and to take his degree, rather than observe the official Catholic rule that undergraduate converts should not return to the University. He invited Hopkins to stay at the Oratory over Christmas and offered him a teaching post. His family were distressed but to their credit and his were reconciled within a short time. No doubt his conversion crisis was linked to some extent with his emotional involvement with Dolben and Addis. Dolben intended to convert but died; Addis converted but married and became denominationally omnivorous. Hopkins taught at the Oratory for two terms, also visiting the Continent. He was now contemplating the priesthood and distressed by his mother's objection. On 12th February he writes to his friend Baillie:

> You know I once wanted to be a painter. But even if I could I wd. not I think, now, for the fact is that the higher and more attractive parts of the art put a strain upon the passions which I shd. think it unsafe to encounter. I want to write still and as a priest I very likely can do that too, not as freely as I shd. have liked, eg. nothing or little in the verse way, but what wd. best serve the cause of my religion.

Complaints about health or lack of energy crop up now and later; they are common enough with sensitive younger people facing some decision or crisis. From 27th April to 7th May 1868 he made a retreat at the Jesuit Manresa House at Roehampton, overlooking Richmond Park. By 12th May he had decided to become a Jesuit. On 11th May he made the decision to burn his poetry manuscripts.[6, 7] Storey[8] argues that little was lost, drafts of known poems mainly; yet it is evidence of his resolve "to write no more, as not belonging to my profession, unless it were by the wish of my superiors."[9] Tragic as it may seem for a poet to write nothing between 24 and 31 he appears to have kept this vow of creative abstinence till the dam burst and he responded to the wreck of the "Deutschland" in December 1875. As it happens he had already given much thought to prosodic and related philosophical/aesthetic questions, and aspects of his studies during the next years could be made to bear upon it, but for the moment his mind was single. On 7th September 1868 he entered Manresa House as a Jesuit novice. The basic novitiate occupied an exact two years, the house being named after the town where St Ignatius Loyola composed his *Spiritual Exercises*. The grounds bordered Richmond Park and were close to Wimbledon Common. Of this Hopkins took full advantage. In his journal for February 1870, he writes:

> On the grass it (the snow) became a crust lifted on the heads of the blades. As we went down a field near Caesar's Camp I noticed it before me *squalentem* (stiff, crusted), coat below coat, sketched in intersecting edges bearing "idiom" all down the slope:- I have no other words yet for that which takes the eye or mind in a bold hand or effective sketching or in marked features or again in graphic writing, which not being beauty or true inscape yet gives interest and makes ugliness even better than meaninglessness. On the Common the snow was channelled all in parallels by the sharp driving wind and upon the tufts of grass (where by the dark colour showing through it looked greyish) it came to turret-like clusters or like broken shafts of basalt. - In the Park in the afternoon the wind was driving little clouds of snow-dust which caught the sun as they rose and delightfully took the eyes: flying up the slopes they looked like breaks of sunlight fallen through ravelled cloud upon the hills and again like deep flossy velvet blown to the root by breath which passed all along. Nearer at hand along the road it was gliding over the ground in white wisps that between trailing and flying shifted and wimpled like so many silvery worms ...[10]

The quotation gives some idea of the richness and exactness of Hopkins' observation and record, linked as it was to emotional response, metaphoric originality and, in parallel with his poetry, linguistic ability. Its contribution to his poetry is clear, and it evidences why he might have become a painter. The *Spiritual Exercises* on which he meditated during the strict regimen of his novitiate open with these words: "Man was created to praise, reverence and serve God our Lord, and by doing so to save his soul." Hopkins' commentary on the Exercises includes a passage on "self-being" telling in its bearing on his mental preoccupations and his poetry. He argues that such "distinctive being" (as Graham Storey puts it) as is in creation can only have been created by "one of finer or higher pitch and determination than itself",[11] thus predicating God's existence and activity. It is easy to see how this aspect of his Jesuit meditations ties in with his developing concepts of "inscape" and "instress". "Inscape" is basically the "selfhood" or "individuality" of an object - the qualities which distinguish it from others. "Instress" may be summarised as the energy or stress that contributes to an object's selfhood or undergirds it, and which communicates that selfhood to our perceptions. It is significant that Hopkins was to find Duns

Scotus the most rewarding of the scholastics for his emphasis on the "this-ness" (or "self-hood") of an object. It is possible then to see that for the poet latent in Hopkins the seven lean years were not without fruit, for it was in them that he (a) created a pent-up emotional reservoir ready to discharge with great force (as it did, at famine's end, with the "Deutschland" poem); (b) observed and recorded; (c) developed his philosophical and prosodic ideas, in particular (d) his concept of "sprung rhythm", which is only a way of saying that he scans, counts or measures by stresses and not by feet, so that one stress may be accompanied by several unstressed syllables or none, so long as the pattern of *stressed* syllables is regular and satisfying. It is true that he does this in a rather complicated way, made to seem more esoteric by the almost musical notation he gives to his "scores"[12] reminding us again that he might have become a musician. Of perhaps greater value was the related attention he gave to the stressing of one word against another (much as a painter might weigh the match of his colours), the effect contributing arguably (in his case) to an impression of strength rather than grace. He was to profit later from his study of Welsh poetry with its complex *cynghanedd* structures, combining alliteration and internal rhyme in given patterns. In "Hurrahing in Harvest", written in Wales, September 1st 1877. the "outcome of half an hour's extreme enthusiasm", after a day's fishing, we find the "this-ness" of "silk-sack clouds" ... "wilful-wavier/ Meal-drift moulded ever and melted across skies ..."; the alliteration and beauty of "l" sounds, a combined marvel of sound-and-meaning in which strength in delicacy "glean(s)" and shows Christ, the centre of so many of Hopkins' poems, whether they are complaint, lament, prayer, or paean of praise as here. But this "harvest" was still to come.

His two years at Roehampton came to an end. On 8th September 1890 he took his vows of poverty, chastity and obedience and left for Stoneyhurst College, in the Pennine foothills, six miles from Blackburn. He enjoyed the wilder countryside, but bouts of ill-health or "sobbing" resulted from excessive fasting and scrupulousness, or sheer pent-up emotional response. Scrupulous and intellectual as he was, Hopkins was Romantic to the core, driven by his devotion to Jesus but also by subjective and ambiguous emotions involving aspiration and self-fulfilment of more than one kind. He was of course a Pre-Raphaelite in Jesuit armour and one thinks of D G Rossetti's poignant lines: "the soul's effluence came to be/ its own exceeding agony".[13] At Stoneyhurst he studied philosophy for three years but he wrote no poetry. From 1873 to '74 he was back at Roehampton where he taught classics and literature, but wrote no poetry. On 28th August, 1874, however, he arrived at St Beuno's College, near St Asaph in North Wales, for three years that were to be amongst his most fecund and happiest. The college was cold; he found his studies in theology taxing, but responded elatedly to the scenery. After his first bathe in St

Winefred's Well, he wrote:

> The strong unfailing flow of the water and the chain of cures from year to year all these
> centuries, took hold of my mind with wonder at the bounty of God in one of his saints ... even
> now the stress and buoyancy and abundance of the water is before my eyes.

Though he drafted an unfinished piece on St Winefred's Well, the real result was to be "The Wreck of the Deutschland" (Dec 1875 - Jan '76) and the sonnets of 1877. In August 1877 he was to write: "No sooner were we among the Welsh Hills than I saw the hawks flying, and other pleasant sights soon to be seen no more." In the magnificent "Windhover" (Penguin 13) note the *cynghanedd sain* with its rhyme/rhyme/alliteration pattern in the final line: "*Fall, gall* themselves, and *gash gold*-vermilion," and feel how the whole thing moves, lifts, floats on the wing, "rebuff(s)" the thrust of the wind, in his unique manner.

That was from the "harvest" of 1877 but it was not until December 1875, when he was 31, that the dam had burst and the lean years had ended. The cause was the loss of the "Deutschland" on the sands of the Kentish Knock, off Harwich on 7th December 1875, her passengers including five nuns who were exiles as a result of Bismark's colleague Falk's anti-Catholic legislation which, amongst other things, excluded them from their former teaching role. To this day many aspects remain intriguing. The captain was experienced. How did he get so close to the notorious banks? It is true there was a blinding snowstorm and he may have miscalculated the strength of the tide, but could the instruments have been tampered with? Soon after the ship struck the propeller was lost. Was this an accident or sabotage? Anti-German as well as anti-Catholic feeling was rife. There were those who thought Britain should have sided with France in the Franco-Prussian War. "The Schiller" had been lost in British waters only the previous year, and on the Saturday following the "Deutschland's" loss there was an explosion on the quay at Bremen that rocked "The Mosel". Why did none of three lightships see her signals or act on them and no boat go out to them for over 30 hours? It is true conditions were appalling and that to have gone out could have been to risk further life, but (to their honour) lifeboat crews do not always take such a calculated view. One of the most wretched aspects is that the dead were robbed by the crews of the very fishing smacks which had not attempted their rescue. Four of the nuns drowned in their cabin; Henrica Fassbender, their tall gaunt leader, was washed overboard. The report in *The Times*, however, said that the Sisters "clasped hands and were drowned together, Henrica calling out loudly "O Christ come quickly"", and it was from this source that Hopkins took his details and inspiration.[14]

> I was affected by the account", Hopkins wrote, "and, happening to say so to my rector, he said
> that he wished someone would write a poem on the subject. On this hint I set to work and
> though my hand was out at first produced one. I had long had haunting my ear the echo of a
> new rhythm which I now realized on paper ... I had to mark the stresses in blue chalk, and this
> ... could not but dismay an editor's eye. so that when I offered it to our magazine The Month,

though at first they accepted it, after a time they withdrew and dared not print it. Robert Bridges called it "presumptuous juggling" and suggested alterations; yet its hard-won affirmation and rhetorical magnificence (for which one has to go back to Donne or Crashaw or forward to Dylan Thomas, for anything like an equivalent) rewards those who will let it work in them, and will read it aloud. It is in two parts, a *preamble*: "over again I feel thy finger and find thee", "the hurtle of hell", "I kiss my hand/ to the stars, lovely-asunder/ Starlight ..." in ten stanzas, and a *narrative* in twenty-five stanzas (each of eight lines though their length and complexity may make them appear longer), with a wonderful series of variations within its pulse and its unity:

> Into the snows she sweeps,
> Hurling the haven behind,
> The Deutschland, on Sunday; and so the sky keeps,
> For the infinite air is unkind,
> And the sea flint-flake, black-backed in the regular blow,
> Sitting Eastnortheast, in cursed quarter, the wind;
> Wiry and white-fiery and whirlwind-swivelled snow
> Spins to the widow-making unchilding unfathering deeps" (Stanza 13)

– but its effect is, of course, cumulative, and it should be read as a whole.[15]

On 23rd September 1877 he was ordained priest and embarked on a series of duties that took him all over Britain; it was a marvel that he found it possible to write poetry at all, during this onerous itinerary. For a short while he was at St Mary's College, Chesterfield; then he was select preacher at Farm Street, London, for a few months. For ten months, 1878-9, he was priest at St Aloysius's, Oxford. Being in Oxford again produced one or two poems: "Binsey Poplars", "Duns Scotus Oxford", "Henry Purcell", and "The Bugler's First Communion", but he didn't hit it off too well parochially. By October 1879 he was on the temporary staff of St Joseph's, Bedford Leigh, near Manchester; then for eighteen months priest at St Francis Xavier's, Liverpool. It was here he was moved to write "Felix Randall" on 28th April 1880, a sonnet which shows his compassion, reveals him writing as a priest and pastor, and with its "bright and battering sandal" earths his more elaborate soarings.

By the autumn of 1881 he was on the staff of St Joseph's, Glasgow; then followed ten months back at Manresa House. He started several projects there, few of which came to fruition, but "the time will come for my verses", he wrote to R W Dixon on December 1st 1881. From autumn 1882 till February 1884 he taught classics at Stoneyhurst, where the rector encouraged him in his writing. In 1883 he met and began a correspondence with that intriguing, now rather neglected fellow-Catholic poet, Coventry Patmore,[16] with whom he enjoyed a most courteous relationship. "Your poems are a good deed done for the Catholic Church and ... the British Empire", Hopkins wrote to Patmore (4.6.86). Patmore, for his part, could see the "gold" embedded in Hopkins' "quartz" but found the "Deutschland" poem as difficult "as Browning".

From February 1884 till his death in June 1889, Hopkins was Professor of Greek at University College, Dublin. Like Newman when he was in Dublin in the 1850's, Hopkins was unhappy there; as unhappy as he had been happy in Wales. His high sounding title boiled down to the conducting and marking of six examinations a year, with up to 500 candidates each time, besides the actual teaching the post involved. This regime drained his health and spirits, an effect exacerbated by the insanitary and drab buildings in which he was housed, which may have been the actual cause of his death.[17] There was a sense of being an alien, too, and no doubt other psychological tensions. It is significant that the main fruits of his time there were the so-called "terrible" sonnets of 1885, (Penguin 41-6) some of which he says were "written in blood":

I wretch lay wrestling with (my God!) my God.

No worst, there is none ...
O the mind, mind has mountains; cliffs of fall ...
        ... Hold them cheap
May who ne'er hung there ...

To seem the stranger lies my lot ...
        ... dark heaven's baffling ban ...

        ... God's most deep decree
Bitter would have me taste: my taste was me ...

These are pearls "oystered from a tear",[18] compact splendours wrought out of dereliction. The last two sonnets completed before his death show an austere calm by comparison, though there is still a Job-like aspect to them. Some two or three late sonnets of Coleridge are not dissimilar in mood. "Birds build - but not I build", says Hopkins in (Penguin 51) "Thou art indeed just, Lord, if I contend/ With thee", or "My winter world, that scarcely breathes that bliss" in (Penguin 52) "To R.B."

Hopkins died in Dublin of typhoid fever on 8th June 1889, and was buried in Glasnevin Cemetery. The Person of Christ was ever before him, both in His own Person, in Nature, and in the people round him. We see this in the theologically striking lines in the "kingfisher" poem (Penguin 34):

... the just man
Acts in God's eye what in God's eye he is -
Christ - for Christ plays in ten thousand places,
Lovely in limbs, and lovely in eyes not his,
To the Father, through the features of men's faces.

– and his last words were, "I am so happy".

"What I do is me: for that I came" he wrote in the same poem, and we could wish he had had longer to do it, yet in what he did he did us proud. His best poetry is urgent, intense, personal - "necessary", as Kandinsky would have put it. It is born of inner necessity and so speaks to the "in-ness" of readers today, as surely as when he wrote it. His life was not long; his body of work small; his poems are short, for the most part, yet his proportion of targets hit is high. Neglected and misunderstood as he was in his lifetime - though he knew happiness, achievement and kindness, as well as frustration and sadness - many would now regard him as one of the most rewarding and enduring of 19th century poets.[19,20]

Notes

1 The National Portrait Gallery has her sketch of him, done when he was 14.

2 Now 9 Oak Hill Park, it has a plaque.

3 Where Betjeman was to show his poems to one T S Eliot.

4 We speak from experience.

5 Poem 44 in the Penguin (W H Gardner) edition. Robert Martin and Graham Storey draw attention to the point.

6 A decision more often taken by a poet's wife, one imagines (?)

7 No wonder he was to advise Patmore similarly in the case of the prose text "Sponsa Dei".

8 Storey, G. *A Preface to Hopkins*. 2nd ed. Longman, 1992, 28

9 Letter to Canon Dixon, 5.10.78, Ref 8, 28. (see also Ref.9 Abbott, CC. ed. of Hopkins correspondence, under Patmore essay)

10 Penguin edition, 120-1

11 Something of Keats' "finer tone" and Patmore again here.

12 It is something Pound would have understood, though he avoids such markings.

13 From "Dante at Verona".

14 This account is indebted to Sean Street's *The Wreck of the Deutschland: an historical note*. Interim Press, 1987

15 The bench mark for any later longer poem, perhaps. Hopkins (like Palgrave) also wrote on the loss of the Eurydice, but could not match his earlier piece. Palgrave's poem (in the 1985 selection by the present writer) does not compare so unfavourably with his.

16 For further reference to Patmore, and their relationship, see the Patmore essay that precedes this.

17 CF. *The Hopkins Society Newsletter* (11) Autumn 1995, 11-13

18 Pearce, B.L. "The Proper Fuss", a poem on Virginia Woolf.

19 Based on lectures given at the National Portrait Gallery on 26th January and 6th December, 1994.

20 It is intriguing that, being in Dublin, he knew of Yeats early work and commended it to Patmore. Cf. Hopkins' letters (Ref 9 of Patmore essay), or Hone (Ref 4 of Yeats essay), 49-50

12. ALICE MEYNELL

Alice Meynell (1847-1922) poet, journalist and essayist, wife and mother, friend and inspirer of so many illustrious literary men, was born Alice Christiana Gertrude Thompson on 22nd September 1847 at 8 Castlenau Villas, close to Hammersmith Bridge,[1] and baptised (or blessed) at St Mary's Church, Barnes on May 10th 1848, the same church in which Dickens had signed her parents' marriage register in October 1845. Her mother was Christiana Weller of Liverpool. Her father was Thomas James Thompson, a widower and in his early thirties when he met Christiana. He had been to Trinity College, Cambridge, and in accordance with his grandfather's Will had not followed any profession. His grandfather, who had died when Thomas was an orphan of six, had derived his income from property and interests in Lancashire and the West Indies. Curiously, if Thomas had died prematurely, the beneficiary would have been Edward Moulton Barrett "of Jamaica", hence Browning saying to Wilfred Meynell in 1882, "our wives are kins-women". In 1844 Thomas went to Liverpool with his friend Dickens and attended a gathering at which Christiana played the piano. Thomas's courtship eventually won her, though her parents had wished her to pursue a concert career.

> "I rather encouraged him in it ...", Dickens wrote to Christiana, "for I had that amount of sympathy with his condition which, but that I am beyond the reach ... of the Wings that fanned *his* fire, would have ... run him through the body ... with good sharp steel.[2]

> "Ask her to save the dress ... Let it be laid up in lavender ... a household God, Immortally Young and Perpetually Green", he had written to Thomas.[3]

Her father provided most of Alice's education. Much of her early life was spent in France and Italy. Francis Thompson (no relation) testifies that she knew Latin, Greek, Italian, French and German, and was familiar with art, music, poetry,[4] so her father had done his work well with a gifted pupil. Her elder sister Elizabeth (1846-1933) was to become Lady Butler and achieve early fame as a painter of battle scenes such as "The Roll Call", "Inkermann" and "Scotland for Ever", attracting the patronage of Queen Victoria. There is thus this distinct contrast between the painter, who achieved considerable fame but is scarcely remembered now,[5] and her sister Alice, who must have seemed in her shadow for much of her life, and who did not become Lady anything, but has left us poetry, essays, *and* the sense of a presence, the appreciation of which has continued to grow. Deeply reflective as she was by nature, evidently she was as happy and adaptable as a child as when a grown woman. What she felt and thought when young we can only glean from her work:

> If any of the three -
> Parents and child - believe they have prevailed
> To keep the secret of mortality,

I know that two have failed.[6]

Her mother became a Catholic about 1870 and Alice followed suit some two years later, the step emphasising those devout, self-abnegating elements of her nature from which it arose. Her piety and modesty will have influenced the restricted scope she gave to her Muse, as in the case of the Anglican Christina Rossetti, yet that there was nothing sanctimonious or glum about her we know from many testimonies, not least that of Coventry Patmore's light-hearted lines, written at a later period:

> With a laugh like many primroses
> She flies the children's chase;
> And she comes in to breakfast
> As light as a May morning ...

– while Victoria Sackville-West says that, though her voice was contralto, her laughter was high and light.

Her first book of poems *Preludes* came out in 1875, when she was 28, two years before her marriage. Aubrey de Vere brought her work to the attention of Tennyson and Sir Henry Taylor, and they, with Patmore, Ruskin, and Rossetti, encouraged her in its publication. This earlier writing, religious and reflective as it was, and marked by a certain sensuosity of great restraint and purity, was influenced by the English Romantic poets and encouraged, too, by an abortive friendship with a young Catholic priest with whom she had enjoyed great empathy. The parting from him, which both realised was unavoidable, led to lines which speak to the heart more openly and directly than the later subtle, cerebral, rigorously exorcised work, for which she herself expressed preference. The fact is that they arose from what perhaps was perhaps the most intense attachment of her life,[7] happy as she was in marriage, and much as she was to "inspire" other men.

"Renouncement" (Nonesuch, 61) is well-known:

> I must not think of thee; and, tired yet strong,
> I shun the thought that lurks in all delight ...
> But when sleep comes to close each difficult day ...
> With the first dream that comes with the first sleep
> I run, I run, I am gathered to thy heart.

– "The Garden" (Nonesuch, 60) and "Thoughts in Separation" (Poems, 1923, 21) are sonnets similar in mood and feeling. "A Shattered Lute" (Poems, 27) offers a touching conceit:

> I touched the heart that loves me as a player
> Touches a lyre. ...
>   I stand as mute
> As one with vigorous music in his heart
> Whose fingers stray upon a shattered lute.

In "After a Parting" there is a control and tone that evokes Coleridge or her co-religionist Hopkins, in their poems of related kind:

> Swift are the currents setting all one way;
> They draw my life, my life, out of my heart." (Nonesuch, 62)

Her earlier poems include one of her few longer pieces, "A Letter from a Girl to her Own Old Age", which Ruskin called "perfectly heavenly" but the working out of which she herself thought inferior to the idea. Its more amplified and public manner, its three-(pentameter) lined verses with a common rhyme to a verse, and its proliferation of feminine endings, certainly gives it distinction, however:

> Listen - the mountain winds with rain were fretting,
> And sudden gleams the mountain-tops besetting.
> I cannot let thee fade to death forgetting. ...
>
> Only one morning, and the day was clouded. ...

– and the coda beautifully recalls its start, as she speaks of:

> The one who now they faded features guesses,
> With filial fingers they grey hair caresses ... (Nonesuch, 50-52)

In 1877, the year she was thirty, she married Wilfred Meynell (1852-1948), Catholic editor and journalist. His family came from Yorkshire and he was descended on his mother's side from the Tuke family, notable for their part in the anti-slavery movement, and their work in ameliorating the lot of the insane. The marriage appears to have been a happy one, harmonious in its family life and partnership in journalistic work, restrictive as that work may have been to the full expression of her powers or, having regard to her deference to husband and Church, to the free play of her thought - whilst a family of eight children cannot but impose its restraints. "No single act of hers in life or literature was not pledged", when she "chose" the "law" of her adopted Church, wrote her daughter Viola.[8] "Thoughts yet unripe in me I bend one way", she writes in "The Young Neophyte" (Nonesuch, 59). It is the same spirit that we find in many Victorian Christian writers. It can be inhibiting, crippling. In a poet like Hopkins it is the very source and foundry of his strength, the furnace from which he draws his force, the well from which he rebounds renewed, that devotional self-limiting or *kenosis* that re-shapes his energies, and which appears to those who have never experienced it to be pure waste. It is the very reticence and purity of Alice Meynell's work which gives it authority, discloses another dimension to reality, and draws her readers to it, without question. Yet we must regret the amount of her time taken up with unrewarding, debilitating labour; the lack of opportunity to be "fallow", the sense of some gusto lost, the comparative smallness of her poetic oeuvre which suggests, whatever the kindness, acquiescence, and happy fruitfulness of all concerned, that there has been some "restraint of trade". George Moore was of that opinion, yet the form of her life and work may have been the natural expression of her mature nature. At any rate, journalism became her main occupation. She assisted Wilfred not only by supplying essays and reviews for the journals of which he was editor, but by proof-reading and other related labour. At the same time, she was contributing to other periodicals. She assisted Wilfred in regard to *The Pen* (1888, short-lived), *The Weekly Register* (1881-98), and *Merry England*, a monthly (1883-95), contributing essays on Tennyson, Ruskin, Browning, Rossetti, Swinburne, George Eliot, Patmore and the Carlyles. She contributed to the *Dublin Review* from 1906 to the year of her death, and to the *Scots Observer* (subsequently *National Observer*) from 1889 to 1894, under the trenchant editorship of W E Henley. Her first volume of essays *The Rhythm of Life* (1893) was drawn from these journals. There is a distinction in the thought and phrasing of these pieces however unassuming each may appear on the surface. Consider this from the title essay:

> The souls of certain of the saints, being singularly simple and single, have been in the most complete subjection to the law of periodicity. Ecstasy and desolation visited them by seasons. They endured, during spaces of vacant time, the interior loss of all for which they had sacrificed the world. They rejoiced in the uncovenanted beatitudes of sweetness alighting in their hearts. Like them are the poets whom, three times or ten times in the course of a long life, the Muse has approached, touched, and forsaken. And yet hardly like them; not always so docile, nor so wholly prepared for the departure, the brevity, of the golden and irrevocable hour, Few poets have fully recognised the metrical absence of their Muse. For full recognition is expressed in only one way - silence.

– or this on "Rain":

> The long stroke of the raindrop, which is the drop and its path at once, being our impression of a shower, shows us how certainly our impression is the effect of the lagging, and not the haste, of our senses. What we are apt to call our quick impression is rather our sensibly tardy, unprepared, surprised, outrun, lightly bewildered sense of things that flash and fall, wink, and are overpast and renewed, while the gentle eyes of man hesitate and mingle the beginning with the close. These inexpert eyes, delicately baffled, detain for an instant the image that puzzles them, and so dally with the bright progress of a meteor, and part slowly from the slender course of the already fallen raindrop, whose moments are not theirs.

How similar, that to the passage from Hopkins notebooks on the snow, or the observant precision of so much of Virginia Woolf's work, in the exact, delicate reflectiveness of its description.[9] I like her suggestion in "Shadows" that we should leave the walls "blank, unvexed, and unencumbered with paper patterns", so that the shadows might play upon them from the "handful of long sedges and rushes in a vase" with "their slender gray design." Her essays on "Clouds", "Landscape", "Solitude" are equally rewarding, while her moving piece on the wife of Dr Johnson shows great independence of thought, as well as sympathy.

Her friendship with Coventry Patmore has been touched on in the "portrait" devoted to him. It brought late into his life an immense impetus, an intoxicating, illuminating glow, she having previously admired his high-minded mysticism from afar, and he having encouraged her early writing. It may have led each to slightly over-assess the merits of the other's productions. It fed into his prose meditations on the link between Divine and human love, almost inevitably, but was too late to stir him to further poetry of distinction.[10] It brought him happiness - and angst, when she was unable to give him much of her company. It has to be remembered that she will have been in her forties when she got to know him; a woman happily married, with a large family and an immense amount of demanding journalistic work; a woman of absolute propriety and probity, for whom he was not the only man in her life. Apart from the young priest she had known earlier, her husband and Patmore, there was the gentle and vulnerable Francis Thompson, and the poet and novelist George Meredith, of whom Patmore became somewhat jealous, not surprisingly, perhaps, when in her poem "Free Will" she refers to Meredith as "the Master". Yet there *was* great empathy between her and Patmore,[11] and in the study of him we have noted the indications of her regard, including her production of an anthology of his work.[12] Viola sees he and Francis Thompson as in similar case. "In regard to Alice Meynell's self-contained, or family-contained, existence, both men were in outer darkness", she writes.[13] Occasionally the two men were to confess to, and console, each other in their plight, but that is not for us here. What is significant is that this regard, on the part of so many men of gifts and discernment, was not mere infatuation for someone of twenty, but for one who, when Patmore and Thompson were consoling each other, was nearing fifty. It is a tribute to her tact and sensitivity, surely, as much as to her spirituality, her charm, and her intellect.

> How should I gauge what beauty is her dole
> Who cannot see her countenance for her soul?[14]

Her second book of essays *The Colour of Life* (1896), consisting almost entirely of *Pall Mall Gazette* essays, was reviewed by both her ageing champions, Patmore and Meredith, whilst tribute was also forthcoming from Francis Thompson.

From 1890 to 1906 the Meynells lived at 47 Palace Court, a tall, elegant, substantial terraced house close to the NW corner of Kensington Gardens, and it was here that the gifted, dependent figure of Francis Thompson came to haunt the library table at which she was trying to work. What with the children concealed underneath it, as well, it is a wonder that she did not find her task impossible. As it happens it was Wilfred who had the most regard for the poet's work and welfare and arranged, at his own expense, for the latter, even while they were still living at Phillimore Place, close to Holland Park Walk,[15] when the poet's need was great. But Alice, too, appreciated his other-worldliness and ideals and, as is not unknown, undertook much of the day to day burdens of her husband's concern. "Love in Dian's Lap", the sequence dedicated to her in his *Poems* of 1893, aided the advocacy of Patmore and Meredith in securing for her work that prestige which "its own depth and reticence might have longer delayed."[16] In 1893 a second collection of her poetry was published, titled simply *Poems* like Thompson's book. She was now 46. This was followed by *Other Poems*, 1896; *Later Poems*, 1902;[17] *Collected Poems* (1913, -); *Ten Poems*, 1915; *A Father of Women*, 1917; *Last Poems* (posthumously in 1923); then back to *Poems* again, also in 1923. Gradually her work was to become more and more cerebral and restrained; to become, if anything, even shorter and more tangential, elusive, than ever, so that it not infrequently defies (or wards off, initially) our entrance to the emotion that engenders it. It was a slow change, but she herself preferred the later manner, and professed herself content if her earlier work had been withdrawn from circulation. As it was, she insisted that it be given a separate section in collected editions; yet she is at her best, one might suggest, in those poems, from whatever period, in which her innate, if restrained, sensuosity is in some way apparent. In neither the cerebral nor the sensuous category is the unremarkable anthology piece "The Shepherdess" which when her husband said it would make her name she was ready to suppress.

> She walks - the lady of my delight -
> A shepherdess of sheep.
> Her flocks are thoughts. ... (Nonesuch, 13)[18]

Much more seized of her strength is "To the Body":

> Upon thy tongue the peach
> And in thy nostrils breathes the breathing rose (Nonesuch, 5)

– Marvellian, in fact, or "The Rainy Summer":

> The forest, rooted, tosses in her bonds,
> And strains against the cloud ...
>
> Bees, humming in the storm, carry their cold
> Wild honey to cold cells. (Nonesuch, 6)

How varied her work is within its modest compass. There is this restrained but firm response to her senses; the heartfelt honesty, the poignant directness, of the early sonnets; the intellectual or imagistic refinement of "Free Will" or "Reflexions", respectively; the devotional simplicity of "I am the Way" that becomes epigrammatic in "Via, et Veritas ..." ("The way was He.") There are poems of straightforward impression like "November Blue" or "A Dead Harvest" (Nonesuch, 10 & 9) - though there's a brooding undertone to the latter's close - on London scenes which are not so different from some of W E Henley's . There is "Maternity's" spare perception in 8 terse lines, a gem cut with a "chisel", as Sackville-West might put it, fashioned of "craft and integrity". (Nonesuch, 16). Yet where the subject does not rebuke extravagance, there is an almost Keatsian lushness, as in "A Thrush Before Dawn" (Nonesuch, 26-7), reminding us that his work was an early inspiration, as we catch echoes of the "Nightingale" ode:

> Darkling, deliberate, what sings ...[19]
> And first-first loves, a multitude,
> The exaltation of their pain;
> Ancestral childhood long renewed;
> And midnights of invisible rain ...
> This yet remoter mystery? ...
> A graver still divinity? ...

So her work is varied. Yet are not all its best features gathered up in "The Watershed" (Nonesuch, 19) where her perceptive, lyrical and reflective qualities combine, to be summed up in one splendid final image, where it is what she *felt* that is so exultantly communicated:

> I seemed to breast the streams that day;
> I met, opposed, withstood
> The northward rivers on their way,
> My heart against the flood -
> My heart that pressed to rise and reach,
> And felt the love of altering speech.
> Of frontiers, in its blood.
>
> But oh, the unfolding South! the burst
> Of summer! Oh, to see,
> Of all the southward brooks the first!
> The travelling heart went free
> With endless streams; that strife was stopped;
> And down a thousand vales I dropped,
> I flowed to Italy.

All this while she toiled at her journalistic work, writing, editing and proof-reading, whilst attending to her children and being an acceptable hostess. It is not possible to say much here of her "politically" related work, but she was a keen supporter of woman's suffrage, and worked hard on its behalf, whilst not being of a "militant" tendency, characteristically. She and Wilfred also risked social disfavour by their pro-Boer position during the South-African War. Alice's brother-in-law, General Butler, had resigned his Cape Town command at the outbreak of the conflict; had returned to England and suffered a difficult time in consequence. The Meynell integrity was thus not one confined to an ivory tower. There was a break for her in 1901-2 when she had become well enough known to lecture in America on such subjects as 17th century poetry; her father's friend, Charles Dickens, and the Brontes. The lectures were well received though she chose not to make it a way of life on her return. In 1905 they moved to (sumptuous) attics above Burns & Oates in Granville Place, which Wilfred had altered and furnished to his taste. Her books of reprinted essays appeared with regularity. *The Children* (1897), *The Spirit of Place* (1899), *Ceres' Runaway* (1909), *Hearts of Controversy* (1917), with essays on Tennyson and Swinburne besides the Brontes and Dickens, and *The Second Person Singular* (1921). She speaks of Dickens' "trust in human sanctity, his love of it, his hope for it, his leap at it. He saw it in a woman's face first met, and drew it to himself in a man's hand first grasped."[20] She notes the "wild quality of purity" in *Wuthering Heights*, and of its author says:

> She contrived to remove herself from the world ... She lends her voice in disguise to her men and women ... (and if) for a moment her reader seems about to come into her immediate presence ... she denies herself to him. ... Wild fugitive, she vanished, she escaped ... exiled by the neglect of her contemporaries, banished by their disrespect ... she might rather have pronounced upon these the sentence passed by Coriolanus ... 'I banish you.'[21]

Of those few prose books initially conceived as books (and not simply collections of essays) most were commissioned by publishers. Her study of *John Ruskin* (1900) reminds us that he had admired her poetry and corresponded with her. *Mary. the Mother of Jesus* (1912) examines the subject as reflected in art, poetry, theology, tradition and morality. More spontaneous enthusiasms were *The Flowers of the Mind*, an anthology of 1897, and *The Poetry of Pathos and Delight* (1895) the selection from Patmore that, published the year before he died, must have given them both satisfaction. She sought to present his more accessible passages rather than those she thought necessarily the best or the most profound. There was also a children's anthology, published posthumously.

She was a mystic in the sense of those gifted people who are given the grace to live out their devotional lives in the full glare of the world (for a Kensington drawing room is not all that different from a Proustian salon, a TV chat show, or the average suburb of the day) showing their devotion by what they do and are. She liked Francis Thompson's poetry best when he made Patmore his model, for it was the aspiration and, indeed, mysticism, of her crotchety devotee that she most admired. Yet in her poetry her expression of her being is almost always reticent, and of a miniaturist character. We do not look to her for abundance of force, but primarily for that *taste* which seems to have distinguished her whole existence, the result of hard work and courtesy, as much as of natural elegance, down to the schooling of her laugh.[22] Even Patmore rather felt she lacked expressive power; a charge which as Herbert Read points out,[23] could certainly have been brought against himself. Should she have had more ambition? Was there something deep down, which never got out? Should she had resisted a little the pressures of faith and commitment? The answer can only be conjectural but is probably: No. We cannot ask every writer to fit the norm of creative activity marked on some clinic of aestheticism's wall. In allowing herself to be the servant of husband, children, faith and society, I think it likely that she rightly, instinctively, followed the dictates of her own nature, though another decision might be right for another, given another temperament, another situation, another time. In "Reflexions" she felt she had succeeded "in singing the highest thought of intellectual passion and emotion" of which she was capable. "It does not matter. If no one cares ... it is written", she added. That was characteristic. "It has my stature, that keen line/ (let mathematics vouch for it) ..." she might have said, as in "Winter Trees on the Horizon" (Nonesuch, 36).

These poems do not shout; they are not on striking or unusual themes. They do not emphasise her femininity; neither do they veil it or deny it. It comes down to taste again; to a sense of balance and aptness; to the spirit in which ideas are conveyed; to a personal modesty and courtesy which is rather out of fashion today,[24] but retains its virtue in every aspect of life. One at least who appreciated her was her husband, Wilfred, who wrote:

> And if you write my epitaph,
> No name or date be there, but rather
> Here lies Her Husband and Their Father.[25]

Just as her reputation has crept up on her sister's and left it behind, so this quiet poetry of Alice Meynell's continues to keep pace with many a better-known name and to find a place in readers' hearts. She died in London on 27th November 1922 but her work, and something of her spirit, surely, lives on.[26, 27]

Notes
1 Now 116 Castelnau – the road that runs from Barnes Common to Hammersmith Bridge.
2 Viola Meynell. *Alive Meynell: a memoir*, 1929 (10, letter of 8.4.1844)
3 Ref. 2, p9 (29.3.1844)
4 Viola Meynell. *Francis Thompson and Wilfred Meynell*, 1952, 48
5 Though her "Eyes Right" painted in response to the Great War, is in St Osmunds, Castelnau.
6 "Intimations of Mortality" (Nonesuch, 40). Her poetry and essays (*Poems*, Burns Oates, complete edition, 1923, etc. eg.) can be found on antiquarian shelves readily enough, but *Selected Poems*, the Nonesuch edition of 1965, edited by Francis Meynell, is perhaps the most accessible edition.
7 There is something in common here with Palgrave's more passionate poems of the early 1850s, written with Georgina Alderson in mind.
8 Ref. 2, 43
9 Amongst my contemporaries Penelope Shuttle, Eric Ratcliffe and the late Marguerite Edmonds have seemed to me to possess this gift, whilst Peter Redgrove has combined it with a psychic energy all his own.
10 We pass over those trifles he wrote in tribute to her. The quotation given earlier in this essay, and those in the Patmore essay, will give adequate idea of them.
11 It is just possible that this, if indeed mutual, was in itself a reason for her "cooling" of the relationship.
12 Had they been able to share their thoughts even a little more, it might have been highly productive for both of them.

13 Cf. Ref. 4, 106-7, 110

14 Francis Thompson. Cf. Victoria Sackville-West. *Alice Meynell: verse and prose*, 1947, 27-34 (31)

15 To Viola, when he first appeared, he was an "unkempt and diseased vagrant", Ref. 2, 70

16 D.N.B.

17 These titles are as inspired as Housman's, especially those edited by Laurence, after A.E.'s death.

18 Her instinct may have been right, one suspects(!)

19 One thinks also of Hardy's "The Darkling Thrush".

20 Cf. Ref. 14, 108-9

21 Cf. Ref. 14, 106-8

22 Yet how she (or any woman similarly placed) could manage all she did, and contrive to live so full and adjusted a life is a mystery. Of course, she will have had the benefit of domestic assistance and of a job which, whilst onerous at times, did not involve commuting or tie her for long and set hours, at an employer's beck, to alien activity. Even so ...

23 Massingham, H.J. & H., eds. *Great Victorians*, (1932?). Herbert Read's essay on Coventry Patmore, 397-410 (404) is extremely perceptive.

24 Not in practice, necessarily, but in the proclamation of ideals.

25 Cf. Ref. 4, 208

26 Based on a lecture given at the National Portrait Gallery on 20th June 1995.

27 I am indebted to Vivian Meynell for the copy of the Nonesuch edition, which he signed when I purchased it in his Chichester bookshop, where it was displayed with a tact equal to the poet's own; and to Benedict Meynell for his courtesy in regard to my lecture.

13. THE PRE-RAPHAELITES

Pre-Raphaelitism, a movement in art which came to involve literature, was initiated by Holman Hunt, Millais, and D G Rossetti in the autumn of 1848. It gathered adherents of the stature of William Morris, Edward Burne-Jones, and Ford Madox Brown, but came to lose much of its identity in the process. In literature, besides artists who wrote (such as Rossetti and Morris), Swinburne, Patmore and Meredith came to be associated with it, albeit tenuously. Ruskin championed it, at Patmore's request. Hopkins has his affinities with it, as has Palgrave's friend, the poet and sculptor Woolner. Pater can be identified with it. In due course it would influence Wilde and Yeats.

The aim of the Pre-Raphaelites was to paint from nature[1], with a clarity, directness, and attention to detail. They tended to use bright, clear colour, and had (in varying degree) religious intention; medievalism came to be associated with the work of some members, but it was the attention to nature which they saw as the significant hallmark of art prior to Raphael, for the movement was essentially a reaction against the conventions of historical and genre painting of the academic sort. They sought more "engagement", an emotional input, or "fervour" as we can call it. In the more claustrophobic, sensuous, medieval aspects of their art, the Keats of "The Eve of St Agnes" and the Tennyson of the Mariana poems or "The Lady of Shalott" can be seen to be forerunners. Of the principle poets, Patmore and Hopkins have been treated as Catholics; Swinburne, a major, undervalued figure, will be considered below. Woolner and the admirable Morris excel in other spheres of creativity; George Meredith's fiction has more resonance than his verse for today.

In the case of Dante Gabriel Rossetti (1828-82) it is more difficult to say whether his art of his writing predominates. His "Hand and Soul" story is a beautiful thing. His poetry includes narratives such as "Dante at Verona" or, more lyrically, "The Blessed Damozel" and "The Stream's Secret"; his "House of Life" sonnet series; his translations of the early Italian poets, and lyrics such as "Even So" or "Sudden Light", the terse objectivity of "The Woodspurge" or the rich depth of "The Orchard Pit". His sonnets have a particular, if claustrophobic vibration, cf. the "Willowwood" sequence, "A Superscription", "Barren Spring", "Autumn Idleness" and "The One Hope". "Ardour and Memory" has a distinct beauty and clarity, with no lack of his characteristic richness of imagery. "Dantis Tenebrae", written in memory of his father, reminds us that he is especially telling, and on his best poetic behaviour, when responding to the associations of the first name he was given. It can be seen in his translations of Dante and his circle, as in the "Dante at Verona" poem already mentioned. "Silent Noon", set by Vaughan Williams; "The Birth-Bond" and "Without Her", are other accessible, yet characteristic sonnets, to the resurgence of which form he greatly contributed. His was a high-souled ardour, and it is sad that circumstance, drug and melancholia, should have polluted its breath. If fervour alone were enough, he could rank beside Hopkins and Tennyson.

His sister's fervour was of another order. Christina Rossetti (1830-1894) was a scrupulous Anglican who refused two suitors, one because he had become a Catholic, the other also on religious grounds but possibly because he seemed more of a friend than a lover. "Goblin Market" is her major poem, and has affinities with Coleridge's "Christabel". Swinburne was amongst its admirers. Besides her lyrics such as "Uphill", "Echo", or "A Birthday", or hymns such as "In the bleak mid-winter" and "Love came down at Christmas", there is a touching immediacy in "My blindest buzzard" or "My love whose heart is tender" and clear-sight in her sonnet "In an Artist's Studio" on her brother's infatuation for Elizabeth Siddall. She has other fine sonnets, too - "Remember" or "An Echo from Willowwood" - that remind us of the similar merits of certain sonnets by Elizabeth Barrett Browning[2], Alice Meynell[3], and Edna Clarke-Hall (née Waugh)[4], better known as an artist.

In her brother, the ardour is almost too intense, and we could wish for a greater objectivity and variety of subject. In Christina, the fire is capped a little, it has to be said, by the very devotion and humility, and welcome sense of irony (cf. "Winter, my Secret") otherwise so commendable. Yet in "A Better Resurrection", "Passing Away" and the confessional yet wry "The Heart Knoweth its own Bitterness" (from which we quote) there is no want of power:

> You scratch my surface with a pin,
> You stroke me smooth with hushing breath ...
> How shall I spend my heart on you ...?
>
> Not in this world of hope deferred,
> This world of perishable stuff:-
> Eye hath not seen nor ear hath heard
> Nor heart conceived that full "enough";
> Here moans the separating sea,[5]
> Here harvests fail, here breaks the heart:
> There God shall join and no man part,
> I full of Christ and Christ of me.

If this has not Hopkins manner, it has matter he would have understood.[6]

Notes
1 "With actuality and probability of detail" Pre-Raphaelitism; edited by James Sambrook. University of Chicago, 1974, 2
2 Cf. her "Sonnets from the Portuguese."
3 Cf. "Renouncement" (etc.) in chapter 12, above.
4 Cf. *Poems* (1926) and *Facets* (1930)
5 Parallels Arnold's "To Marguerite-Continued."
6 Subject of a "Richmond Reading", 30th June, 1994

14. SWINBURNE

Swinburne, one of the most underestimated of major Victorian poets, was himself generous in appreciation, seeing the moral force behind "Goblin Market" and speaking of Christina Rossetti as the Pre-Raphaelite Jael leading her hosts to victory. He ranks next to Browning, Tennyson and Hopkins, in the present writer's opinion, thinking of Yeats as a twentieth century writer. Like Browning, yet in his own distinct manner, with his own range, fecundity and vitality, he is a worthy disciple of Shelley, sharing with the latter his free-thinking, his concern with intellectual freedom *per se*, his rapport with political and philosophical aspirations, and his lofty aesthetic ideals.

Algernon Charles Swinburne (1837-1909) was born in London on 5th April 1837. His mother was a daughter of the 3rd Earl of Ashburnham. Much of his childhood was passed on the Isle of Wight and at his grandfather's seat, Capheaton, in Northumberland on the Scots border. From both these environments, the softer and the rougher, he gained a lifelong love of the sea, often reflected in his work, and it is of interest that his father was an Admiral. On the Isle of Wight his cousin Mary Gordon, a tomboy with literary interests, lived near him. They rode, read, talked and wrote together, and she was *a*, perhaps *the*, central figure in the ultimate loneliness of his emotional life. He learnt French and Italian at his mother's knee. He had the run of his grandfather's library. He went to Eton in 1849, at the age of twelve. His cousin describes him standing there:

> between his father and mother, with his wondering eyes fixed upon me! Under his arm he hugged his Bowdler's Shakespeare, a very precious treasure, bound in brown leather ... He was strangely tiny (probably no more than five feet in height). His limbs were small and delicate; and his sloping shoulders looked far too weak to carry his great head, the size of which was exaggerated by the tousled mass of red hair standing at almost right angles to it. (His voice was) exquisitely soft ... with a rather sing-song intonation.

On a horse he was fearless, and he was a keen, dauntless swimmer in heavy seas. Stoically (or masochistically) he endured beatings at Eton which may have affected the kind of man he became; drank with the rest, and was to acquire bohemianism, republicanism, and atheism - the last named position veering little with the years. After four years at Eton he was taken away for private tutoring, and went up to Balliol College, Oxford, in 1856, at the age of 19. At Oxford he met D G Rossetti, William Morris, and Edward Burne-Jones, who were decorating the Union walls with Arthurian murals, and came under Pre-Raphaelite influence, as well as that of the Elizabethan tragedians. By 1860 Jowett was uneasy about his continued presence at Balliol. He was not "sent down", but left without taking a degree. In the same year he published two Pre-Raphaelite - and Elizabethan - influenced plays, *Rosamund* and *The Queen Mother*. He became close to Rossetti, joining him for a time at 16 Cheyne Walk,

Chelsea, and Rossetti had considerable influence on his work at this period. Articles, lyrics and one or two stories ensued. Some twenty connected tales were intended and it is a pity that more were not completed and that he did not pursue the genre with greater resolution.[1] He met Richard Monkton Milnes and Richard Burton, neither of whom were a helpful influence, and began to drink a good deal. Autumn 1863 to early 1864 was to prove a key period, productive of some of his finest work. His eldest and favourite sister, Edith, died of consumption on 23rd September 1863, and after the funeral Swinburne went to stay with the Gordons at Northcourt, Shorwell, Isle of Wight. Out of loss there came consolatory fruit, for he was able to spend considerable time with his cousin Mary, who was at work on her *Children of the Chapel* (published in 1864) to which he contributed "A Pilgrimage of Pleasure", a play. Here, free of the distractions of London, and under the stimulus of his empathy with his cousin, he could work on *Atalanta in Calydon* and find inspiration for some of his most moving lines; poems that would find their way into the *Poems and Ballad, First Series*, which came out in 1866, his models being Blake, Baudelaire and Shelley, the Greeks, the Elizabethans, and his fellow Pre-Raphaelites. He stayed at Northcourt with Mary until February 1864, and it was there in the Northcourt library that so much of his best work was done, the table strewn with blue sheets of foolscap, whilst Mary practised Handel on the organ. All too soon it became clear that her family had other intentions for Mary, and soon she had married Colonel Disney Leith, a man a good deal older than herself. In the initial angst of finding that he was to lose her (her company and stimulus as well as his emotional hopes) he wrote poems such as "The Sundew" with its close observation:

A little marsh-plant, yellow green,
And pricked at lip with tender red,
Tread close, and either way you tread
Some faint black water jets between
Lest you should bruise the curious head

.... more than we
Is the least flower whose life returns,
Least weed renascent in the sea.

....
O red-lipped mouth of marsh-flower,
I have a secret halved with thee.
The name that is love's name to me
Thou knowest and the face of her
Who is my festival to see. ....

– "A Leave-Taking" ("Let us go hence, my songs; she will not hear"), in which we see elements that could have inspired Ezra Pound, and the magnificent, sustained, almost elegiac "The Triumph of Time", in which he sees his "whole life's love go down in a day":

> I wish we were dead together today ...
> How we should slumber, how we should sleep
> Far in the dark with the dreams and the dews.
> And dreaming, grow to each other, and weep.
> Laugh low, live softly, murmur and muse;
> Yea, and it may be, struck through by the dream,
> Feel the dust quicken and quiver, and seem
> Alive as of old to the lips, and leap
> Spirit to spirit as lovers use.[2]

> Sick dreams and sad of a dull delight;
> For what shall it profit when men are dead
> To have dreamed, to have loved with the whole soul's might,
> To have looked for day when the day was fled?
> Let come what will, there is one thing worth,
> To have had fair love in the life upon earth:
> To have held love safe till the day grew night,
> While skies had colour and lips were red.

– though there is more to the poem than that; so much life, in fact, as in other beautiful works in this collection; "Felise" – "What shall be said between us here / Among the downs, between the trees ..." with its "two gifts" that seem to anticipate T F Powys's "Mr Weston's Good Wine", or the simplicity of "A Match" ("If love was what the rose is, / And I were like a leaf, / Our lives would grow together") and, in a different mood the "Hymn to Proserpine", a remarkable and fine poem, whether or not the reader concur with its message, with something of Browning's manner and historical-impersonational, re-creational approach:

> Thou hast conquered, O pale Galilean; the world has grown grey from thy breath .... the old faiths loosen and fall, the new years ruin and rend. ...

– an approach that recurs yet could have been taken further, one feels, had he not put so much of this side of his imagination into his plays.

Atalanta in Calydon was published in 1865, the year before the above poems, and contains those rightly admired and anthologised choruses that first brought him to public attention: "When the hounds of spring are on winter's traces", "Who hath given man speech?", and "Before the beginning of years," the inspiration and control of which it seems we may owe, indirectly as it may be, to Mary Gordon.

Early in 1863 he had met Whistler (being nursed through an illness by that well-known figure in art history, Whistler's mother) and, having had to part from Mary Gordon early in 1864, he met Landor and Mrs Gaskell in Italy. In 1867-8 there came his bizarre, short-lived relationship with Adah Menken, the Jewish-American actress. In 1868 he published his critical appreciation of William Blake, and in 1871, the year he was 34, the *Songs Before Sunrise*, an apotheosis of the republican cum Romantic spirit, inspired not only by Shelley but by his admiration for the Italian patriot Mazzini. The best poems in this book, such as "Hertha" or "Genesis", extend his range beyond Italy, or the personal, following on from the "Hymn to Proserpine" or the "Who hath given man speech?" chorus. Some telling lines from the close of "Hertha" give an indication of its theme:

> Behold now your God that ye made you, to feed him with faith of your vows ...
> For behold, I am with you, am in you and of you; look forth now and see ...
> Even love, the beloved Republic, that feeds upon freedom and lives ...
> Man, pulse of my centre, and fruit of my body, and seed of my soul ...
> Man, equal and one with me, man that is made of me, man that is I

– In "Genesis there is the glint of duality and of "Mr Weston's Good Wine" again:

> For in each man and each year that is born
> Are sown the twin seeds of the strong twin powers;
> The white seed of the fruitful helpful morn,
> The black seed of the barren hurtful hours.

"The Eve of Revolution", which he considered the key poem of the volume, has echoes of the four horsemen of the Apocalypse and of Browning's Childe Harold in its four times repeated: "I set the trumpet to my lips and blow." "On the Downs" is a beautiful lyric, on familiar territory, where:

> .... on the lip's edge of the down,
> Here where the bent-grass burns to brown
> In the dry sea-wind, and the heath
> Crawls to the cliff-side and looks down,
> I watch, and hear beneath
> The low tide breathe.

Tragedies continued to appear: "Chastelard" in 1865, "Bothwell" in 1874 and "Erechtheus" in 1876, "Mary Stuart" in 1881, with others to follow. 1877 was a key year for his fiction for from it stem *Lesbia Brandon*, a substantial fragment, never completed, and *A Years' Letters*. published in *The Tatler* in instalments in 1877 and published subsequently as *Love's Cross Currents*. In 1862 he had published "Dead Love", and three or four other pieces saw print at the time of his death. It was also 1877 that saw his *A Note on Charlotte Bronte*, whilst in July he was reputedly poisoned by the lilies with which a too enthusiastic hostess had filled his bedroom, and did not recover fully until the November. One suspects that the heavy drinking he was indulging in by now had something to do with it. He was often in something of a stupor, and a condition akin to epilepsy has been suspected. Yet in 1878, the year he was forty-one, his *Poems and Ballads, Second Series*, appeared, containing some of his finest work. There is the moving "Inferiae" on his father's death, which closes:

> The life, the spirit, and the work were one
> That here - ah, who shall say, that here are done?
> Not I, that know not; father, not thy son,
> For all the darkness of the night and sea.

– the nearest he gets to converting atheism to agnosticism, perhaps. There are the Villon translations, vigorous and colloquial in phrase and refrain: the "pray to God that he forgive us all" of the ballad Villon wrote when expecting to be hanged[3], or the:

> ...fierce old age with foul bald head ...
> Foul flapping ears like water-flags;
> Peaked chin, and cheeks all waste and dead,
> And lips that are two skinny rags:
>
> Thus endeth all the beauty of us ...

of "The Complaint of the Fair Armouress". There is "The Forsaken Garden", that lament for a garden slipping into the sea, on the coast of the Isle of Wight, that Swinburne had known as a boy:

> So long have the grey bare walks lain guestless,
> Through branches and briars if a man make way.
> He shall find no life but the sea-wind's, restless
> Night and day.

There is "Ave Atque Vale", the beautiful poem on the death of Baudelaire, actually written a few months earlier than the event it commemorates, on receiving false information that Baudelaire had died. It lies somewhere between Shelley's "Adonais" and Arnold's "Thyrsis"; closer to the former in mood and achievement, but less consolatory than either:

> Yet with some fancy, yet with some desire,
> Dreams pursue death as winds a flying fire,
> Our dreams pursue our dead and do not find.
> Still, and more swift than they, the thin flame flies,
> The low light fails us in elusive skies,
> Still the foiled earnest ear is deaf, and blind
> Are still the eluded eyes.

It was in 1879, scarcely a year after these poems were published, that his self-appointed guardian Theodore Watts-Dunton "rescued" him from a detrimental lifestyle that was undoubtedly working havoc with him, and took him to live with him at No. 2 (now No. 11) The Pines, Putney Hill, in the SW suburbs of London. Swinburne was 42, with thirty years before him. Up to then his proud temperament had never quite settled either to revolt and assert itself or to submit. Now, and too early, he chose submission; the force went out of him, and the result (the best possible from a magistrate's, doctor's, or suburban householder's point of view) was a loss both to English poetry and (very possibly) to its fiction. The association of his former friends was often detrimental, doubtless, but stimulating creatively. The influence of Watts-Dunton, though well-meant, and of signal advantage to body and soul, did nothing for the poet's creative well-being and artistic afflatus. Indeed, he became an over-zealous guardian who kept him as far as possible from his former friends, and so denied him the company of mettlesome peers. It is significant, perhaps, that his 1880 publication *The Heptalogia* consisted of parodies of Tennyson, E B Browning, D G Rossetti and, not for the last time, of himself, cf. "Nephelidia" with its blushes that "thicken and thrill as a theatre thronged at appeal of an actor's appalled agitation". In the same year he published his Study of *Shakespeare*, a further contribution to his sympathetic and illuminating critical oeuvre, stemming from his wide reading (in several languages), responsive enthusiasm and clear-eyed perceptions. His response to Blake and Charlotte Bronte has already been noted. His defence of his own and Rossetti's work was masterly:

Art can never be the handmaid of religion, exponent of duty, servant of fact, pioneer of morality", he writes. "With these callings she refuses to act, and she remains inviolate. Though you were to bray her in a mortar she will maintain her integrity.[4]

In his prose - and throughout his career -", writes Robert L Peters, "Swinburne insisted repeatedly that the details of a poem or painting (what Coleridge called "fixities" and "definites") be integral to the work of art as a whole. Verbal and decorative encrustations, pretty scenarios lavished up and down a poem or over a picture, and an exaggerated "scientific" literalism *prevent*, he thought, the creation of great art. The purple passage and the nervously literal scene must be organic to the overall form of the work; we must not be "vexed or fretted by mere brilliance of point or sharpness of stroke, and such intemperate excellence as gives astonishment the precedence of admiration: such beauties as strike you and startle and go out"[5]

1882 saw the publication of *Tristram of Lyonesse*, a response in large measure to Tennyson's *Idylls of the King*, Swinburne speaking scornfully of "Morte d'Arthur" as "Morte d'Albert". It was a work he had actually projected much earlier, cf. his letter to Edward Burne-Jones of 4th November 1869:

The Thought of your painting and Wagner's music ought to abash but does stimulate me: but my only chance I am aware will be to adhere strongly to Fact and Reality - to shun Fiction as perilously akin to lying, and make this piece of sung and spoken History a genuine bit of earnest work in these dim times. I have just been doing the storm that overtakes them when Tristram rows so hard and gets a thirst.[6]

His *Century of Roundels* (1883) contains the pleasant title poem on the form in question and "Ventimiglia", a modern-sounding poem:

The sky and sea glared hard and bright and blank ...
More deep, more living, shone her eyes that drank
The breathless light and shed again on me ...[7]

In 1884 he published *A Midsummer Holiday* with "In Sepulcretis", which says leave dead writers and private lives alone, still a relevant message today, and one with which Browning and Palgrave would have agreed, since they each have similar poems. The sonnet "Solitude" shows yet again how wonderfully he responds to the sea and the coast.

From the *Poems and Ballads, Third Series* (1889) comes "A Reiver's Neck Verse", a dialect piece reminding us that he came from Northumberland and the Border country, and could manage more styles than one:

> Some die sailing, and some die wailing,
> And some die fair and free:
> Some die flyting, and some die fighting,
> But I for a fause love's fee, my dear,
> But I for a fause loves's fee.

The Sisters (1892) is yet another of his poetic tragedies. It ends in melodrama but it has subtler material which in some ways anticipates Eliot's manner in his later plays. There are autobiographical elements in it, since he returns for one last time (though he was only 55) to the Mary Gordon story. It is an interesting date (1892)[8] because in that year her husband Disney Leith died, and she and Swinburne resumed correspondence, using a childish kind of cipher they had used years earlier. She was three years younger than Swinburne so at this juncture would have been 52. In "By the North Sea" (1880) or "A Swimmer's Dream" (November 1889, published 1894) his rival Muse, the coast and sea, once again does not fail him. In section IV, "O russet-robed November" there are affinities with Palgrave's "Autumn" of November 1871 and the Housman of "Tell me not here, it needs not saying" (*Last Poems*, 1922) whose *A Shropshire Lad* was to be published in 1896.[9] In the Spring of 1899 Max Beerbohm visited him at *The Pines* and the wry record of his youthful awe can be read in his paper "No. 2 The Pines" in *And Even Now* (1920). He describes the dark hall, the pictures in Rossetti's manner on the walls, the solid, even "stolid" mid-Victorian room, the gas-brackets, and the suspense of watching the door through which Swinburne would appear, on his return from his morning walk across Putney Heath or Wimbledon Common:

> Here he was ... a strange small figure in grey, having an air at once noble and roguish, proud and skittish ... the immense pale dome of his head ... the eyes of a god, and the smile of an elf ... (He) receded from the waist upwards (leaning back so that) the back of his jacket (hung) far away from his legs; and so small and sloping were his shoulders that the jacket seemed ever so likely to slip right off.

He was short in stature, and by this period extremely deaf. Yet when he spoke Beerbohm found him come alive with a musical outpouring of words, rather as though crossing Putney Heath was like walking through Paradise, and it must have been a moving experience to hear the poet thus enthralled and to realise that he could hear no more of his words than Beethoven could catch of the music he composed. At that moment that he spoke it was as though his genius was rediscovered in the ageing, tamed frame, and Beerbohm saw in his mind's eye the auburn haired precocious child and ardent aspirer who Mary Gordon would have known. There is one particular feature that Beerbohm noted:

> His hands were tiny, even for his size, and they fluttered helplessly, touchingly, unceasingly ... It made me unhappy to see what trouble he had in managing his knife and fork ... this infirmity ... (had) begun before Eton days. The Swinburne family had ... consulted a specialist, who said that it resulted from "an excess of electric vitality", and that any attempt to stop it would be harmful ... I have known no man of genius who had not to pay, in some affliction ... either physical or spiritual, for what the gods had given him ...

The years passed now with little variation or interruption. In 1902 he was 65. His poems continued to appear – indeed, there would be a fair number of posthumously published pieces – but most of his "Pines" work was pallid, politically-correct, fugitive stuff, written at the instigation of Watts-Dunton for periodical publication, and a far cry from the verve of his earlier republicanism or personally passionate rhetoric, in which emotion, intellect, and craftsman's cunning of the highest order had combined. He did touch once more on his themes of swimming and the sea in *A Channel Crossing* (1904) but "The Lake of Gaube" concerns an experience of many years before and the title poem is arguably less forceful than the prose account of the crossing concerned that (again) he had written years previously. Otherwise, there may be echoes of earlier themes but they are not usually of any great merit; it is a (perhaps unexpected) pity that there is not more highly ordered elegiac work on the "Ave Atque Vale" model. Even his parodies were now domestic; take "Disgust":

> This was the consequence, was it, of not going weekly to church?

In 1905 the ageing Watts-Dunton married the youthful Clara Reich, but continued to live at "the Pines", and Swinburne could continue to bestow fatherly affection on Bertie Mason, Watts-Dunton's nephew. It is not entirely the lifestyle we might equate with the author of "Atalanta in Calydon", "The Triumph of Time", "Ave Atque Vale" or "The Eve of Revolution". Yet he *had* written that play and those poems, and didn't need to do more. He had his memories, and his books - his fine library which one afternoon, in the inevitable presence of Watts-Dunton, he had shown Beerbohm - and was entitled to enjoy his walks across Wimbledon Common or, occasionally, along the Richmond Road to Barnes Common or Barnes Green. He died on 10th April, 1909, at *The Pines*, after getting wet through walking across Wimbledon Common. He was buried at Bonchurch on the Isle of Wight. The Vicar had difficulty in steering a course between the views of Swinburne, atheist to the end, who wanted no Christian prayers at his burial, and his more conventional relatives who did want them, naturally. The Vicar was in an impossible position, yet from the fact that he gave both parties equal offence we can deduce that he acted with the utmost sensitivity and impartiality. So was buried the disciple of Shelley who was in turn to influence Hardy, Pound and Yeats, Rupert Brooke, and W S Gilbert, Hopkins and Housman, in varying degree. More recently there has been a renewed interest in his ideas and his symbolism, as opposed to that consummate poetic-musical artistry that, for so many years, from his lifetime to ours, those who have not possessed have sought to denigrate. It so happens that ours is an age that both mistrusts rhetoric and, for the most part, can no longer produce it, but compositional afflatus such as his will be honoured in another generation, if not our own. To the present writer it seems also that his psychological insight, his unusual honesty and high-mindedness, in his best work; the way his fervour is often sustained throughout a very long poem, and, indeed, his sheer variety of fervour, place him amongst the first four or five Victorian poets. His length is one thing that has told against him in our rushed and impatient era. Yet his was a profoundly ardent nature, and appeals to all ages and conditions prepared to appreciate high art in which Romanticism persists. Present on that sad yet fulfilled occasion, by the graveside at Bonchurch in 1909, were Hallam, Lord Tennyson, Clara Watts-Dunton, The Mayor of Newport, Mrs Emery Walker, Miss Maria Rossetti, and the wife of an old friend beloved of Rossetti and many times his model - so that it seems almost like the funeral of the Pre-Raphaelite movement itself - Jenny Morris (née Jane Burden). A message came from Mr and Mrs William Rothenstein and another "With love from the little boy to whom Mr Swinburne used to wave his hand", and there was one other person present in Bonchurch that day, familiar to those who have followed this narrative thus far, disguised as her name was by the language of marital etiquette, *Mrs Disney Leith* – Mary Gordon, in fact.[10, 11]

Notes
1 Though we shall see that he returned to it.
2 For signs of his influence on Rupert Brooke see "The Way that Lovers Use" (1913) or "Blue Evening", written in May, 1909. a month after Swinburne died.
3 Cf. Basil Bunting's "Villon" (1925) in his *Collected Poems*, 2nd ed., Fulcrum, 1970
4 Robert L Peters "Algernon Charles Swinburne and the Use of Integral Detail" in *Pre-Raphaelitism*, ed. J Sambrook, 1974, 206-219 (214)
5 Ref. 4, 206. See also Pater's concern in *Appreciations* with the "architecture" of the literary art, which "foresees the end in the beginning and never loses sight of it, and in every part is conscious of all the rest, till the last sentence does but ... justify the first (Ref. 4, 217)
6 *Swinburne* by Philip Henderson. New York, Macmillan, 1974, 154-5
7 "As to women, I saw at Venice one of the three most beautiful I ever saw (the other two were one at Genoa, the other at Ventimiglia" in the Riviera"). *Algernon Charles Swinburne : Selected Poems*; edited L M Findlay. Fyfield/Carcanet, 1982 (1987), 226 & 268. A very accessible contemporary edition.
8 1892 is also the year the Tennyson died and the question of the next laureate came up. "I am told that Mr Swinburne is the best poet in my dominions", Queen Victoria opined, before her statesmen had time to rally.
9 Housman's "For my funeral" (*More Poems* XLVII), also, has the Swinburne metrical "feel".
10 Based on lectures given at the National Portrait Gallery on 20th January 1993 and 11

January 1995.
11. A tribute to Swinburne's continued appeal is Edith Sitwell's *Swinburne: a selection* of 1960 with its valuable introduction. The selection does not do justice to his range, however, excluding poems such as "Hertha", "Genesis" and the "Hymn to Prosperine" of a strong and individual character, and an element of historical re-creative objectivity, besides "Inferiae" and "The Forsaken Garden", and failing to appreciate the sustained achievement which "The Triumph of Time" represents. But it includes "Ave atque vale" and "Atalanta in Calydon" besides much else, and provides us with a fellow-alchemist's appreciation of his master-chemistry with sounds.

15. THE HUMANISTS

Names that might be linked with Swinburne's, in his Shelleyan atheism, are those of Thomas Hardy, who saw the figures of tragedy as pawns moved by the hand of an indifferent or malign Providence, and A E Housman, author of *A Shropshire Lad*, whose collected poems equal Hardy's in the constancy and "fervour" of a gloom calculated to depress the most sanguine. Against this it has to be emphasised that Hardy's poetry (so much vaster in bulk than Housman's) has its countless moments of illumination and loving affection, a deep appeal of insight and expression, a variety of lyrical structure, and is unfailingly humane, if sometimes gratuitously bleak, so that at his blackest moments we sense the compassion underneath. By virtue of his poetry alone (leaving aside his fiction and *The Dynasts*), he far excels Housman in the range and worth of his achievement. Yet Housman, by taking immense pains, and husbanding his talent, has left us more phrases, poems, and lines that haunt the mind than many of his betters, and has created not only a persona but his own world. Yet it should be remarked how positive Swinburne is, despite the atheism to which he so firmly adhered, compared with the other two writers.

Housman is given separate treatment below. A few words follow about Thomas Hardy (1840-1928).

The world-famous novelist started to write poetry as a young man, but received little encouragement.

> When I failed at fervid rhymes,
> "Shall," I said, "persist I?"[1]

He returned to it on relinquishing novel writing after *Jude the Obscure* – his first collection appeared in 1898 – and continued until the end of his long life.[2,3] Between 1903 and 1908 he published *The Dynasts*, his monumental prose and verse reading-drama of the Napoleonic wars with its frequently "cinematographic" evocations of great personages and nonentities, vast panoramas and close-ups, characters of this world and spirits of the spheres, in which, were it not so entirely unique, there might be seen something of Shelley. It is an epic achievement, but primarily he is a lyric poet immense in flair and compass. With masterly colloquial and lyrical power, quaint, quirky actuality, and honesty (if objectivity) of emotion, he creates ballads, narratives, songs, lyrics, vignettes, miniature dramas, reflective pieces, hymn-like, dance-like poems, "moments of vision" (as he titled a collection), all so seemingly casual, so inevitable-seeming, that we could easily miss their art. Few could manage his simplicity without becoming embarrassing, or produce with such finesse the "sunset touch" (per Browning) that "shakes this fragile frame at eve / With throbbings of noontide,"[4] on a par with the best effects of Browning or Tennyson. Direct, conversational, exact in detail, he roots his poems in earth and ties them firmly to particular locations; evokes scene and mood. Nothing could appear more artless than "To Lizbie Browne", "Budmouth Dears", or "The Dance - Continued", yet each secretes trove that remains with the reader. The latter, indeed, has his characteristic sense of the ongoing history and unison of earth and man that we find, too, in "Transformations", "Proud Songsters", or "While Drawing in a Churchyard". Pleasing technically are "The Sigh" and "Ditty" with their multi-syllable line endings, or that remarkable brilliantly constructed cry from the heart "Simple was I and was young"[5] with its Latinisms, its archaisms and inversions: "Love-lore little wist I"; so simple, and odd-seeming, yet so moving and so eloquent. Such poems have a life of their own, whether read on the page, or heard in Gerald Finzi's haunting settings. In a few phrases, in a poem such as "During Wind and Rain", he evokes family life, the passage of time, happiness, sadness, nostalgia, hope and retrospect, the specific and the universal, using the simplest words and expressions. The poems he wrote in 1912-13 when Emma Gifford, his first wife, died, have a special dimension of nostalgia. They abound in re-creative, evocative, recollective power; affection and remorse, as much as grief, under-girding them. In "The Going", verses 1,3,5 vary in structure from 2,4,6. The effect is to contrast the afflatus and vowel-play of the speaker's Cornish-bound mental travelling, with a certain flatness in keeping with his recall to his bereaved dulled self. At one moment he could:

... think for a breath it is you I see
At the end of the alley of bending boughs
Where so often at dusk you used to be ...

– at the next, the shorter-lined verses have the effect of Tennyson's "Break, break, break" with their:

Never to bid goodbye
Or lip me the softest call ...

or:

Well, well! All's past amend ...

"At Castle Boterel", "The Voice", "I found her out there", are each, quite individually effective; in "Places" he portrays himself:

Nay: one there is to whom these things,
That nobody else's mind calls back,
Have a savour that scenes in being lack,
And a presence more than the actual brings;
To whom to-day is beneaped and stale,
And its urgent clack
But a vapid tale.

"After a Journey" recalls the "Under the Waterfall" poem and Pentargon Bay; the emotion of the recalled scene of empathy being conjured by the sound-energy of the poem through the overall structure, the inspired last line, and the splendid

And the unseen waters' ejaculations awe me

– in which "ejaculations" is so much more expressive of what he felt than "soliloquies", the word he originally wrote. The rhyme with "draw me" works, too, though in other hands it could have proved bathetic. He is a master of rhyme and rhythm, and a master reader of the human heart. We can give thanks that the midwife slapped him at his birth, and coaxed him into life, when the doctor had given him up for dead.[6, 7]

Notes
1 "After Reading Psalm XXXIX, XL, etc." (Simple was I ...), written in the 1870's but published in *Late Lyrics and Earlier* (1922), in the same year as Housman's *Last Poems*.
2 Hardy, Thomas *The Complete Poems*; edited by James Gibson. Macmillan, 1976 (1978), (1002 pages).
3 "To Louisa in the Lane" appeared in 1928 but typically recalls a (non-) event of much earlier and might have been written 50 years previously.
4 "I Look Into My Glass."
5 Cf. Ref. 1
6 Subject of a "Richmond Reading" 18th March, 1993
7 A good study of his fiction is that by Lionel Johnson: *The Art of Thomas Hardy*, John Lane, 1895, done before *Jude the Obscure* had appeared.

16. HOUSMAN

In a London Tube train recently, amid a crush of people, I glimpsed on a panel above me these lines:

What are those blue remembered hills,
What spires, what farms are those? (ASL:XL)

That of course is by A E Housman (1859-1936) and comes from *A Shropshire Lad*, first published in 1896. It shows the haunting persistence of his work in the subconscious of the "tribe" and it is *that* Housman who is considered here, rather than the classical scholar.

A E Housman was born in the Valley House, Fockbury, near Bromsgrove, Worcestershire, on the 26th March 1859. The Shropshire hills formed the western horizon of his childhood memories. His mother died in 1871, when he was 12. From 1860 to 1873 the family home was Perry Hall, but in 1873 they moved to Fockbury House. His father was Edward Housman, a Bromsgrove solicitor, a saddish figure after the death of his wife, and it is significant that "AE" would later have to assist the family with the payment of the mortgage. From Fockbury he could see the hills and county which were to give him the locale and title of his most famous sequence, though it is interesting that a poem such as "Bredon Hill" (ASL:XXI), first drafted in July 1891, before his thoughts had crystallised, concerned a place which is actually on the Worcestershire/Gloucestershire border. He will not have been the last poet, however, to rely heavily on atlas and gazetteer and, even more, as in this instance, on the sound and association of a name that appealed to him. This Worcestershire country was what Edward Elgar knew, and perhaps the same feeling flows through them. Housman was born but two years later than Elgar and died but two years after him. Both were introspective men, with brooding, reflective natures. Elgar's early string pieces, the Enigma Variations and , indeed, so many of his compositions, have the feel of the area, whether or not he was living there at the time they were written. Neither man did much creatively in his last dozen years, once the necessary emotional impetus or support was lacking, though, in the case of Elgar, one feels that inspiration came close, more than once, to being revived. Masefield, whose early life centred on Ledbury, also had characteristics in common with both men.

One of Housman's best-known poems, and a far better example of his use of proper names, is "On Wenlock Edge", where he evokes this scenery of the mind, in which the associations of place and personal or national history converge. It was a favourite of Thomas Hardy's:

The gale, it plies the saplings double,
It blows so hard, 'twill soon be gone:
To-day the Roman and his trouble

Are ashes under Uricon.

Housman went to Bromsgrove School and won a scholarship to St John's College, Oxford. He went up at the age of 18, in October 1877. At Oxford, his intellectual presumption was compounded by his meeting up with Moses J Jackson, for whom he conceived a strong and permanent attachment, intense on his part, but not reciprocated to the same degree. A W Pollard says that Jackson was a safe first in science and didn't need to read a lot in the evening so that, apart from the emotional distraction in itself, Housman may have been encouraged to study less himself and to prefer his favourite classical authors to the set texts, whether of literature, history, or philosophy. It is a significant indication of his attitude that after one lecture from Jowett he did not attend his lectures again. So against all expectation he failed to get a First; felt he had let down his family, but had to return to them in Worcestershire while, through 1881-2 he prepared for the civil service examination, studying, as have so many, in the only room with a fire, the general family living room. For the next 10 - 11 years he worked as a clerk at the Patent Office where, it is worth noting, Moses Jackson already worked. His failure to get a First, and the comparative non-distinction and tedium of his post, provides some explanation for his extreme reserve and, at times, rather unpleasant and sardonic persona. He could be scathing in his scholarly criticism; he did not invite his brother or sister to his lodgings, and in later life could be a most morose and disconcerting guest. Nevertheless, it was to produce that other persona, that of the "Shropshire Lad". He lived for a while with Moses Jackson and Jackson's brother Adalbert in Bayswater, then moved to rooms in Highgate, at 17 North Road, where there is a plaque. The poem "Far in a western brookland" (ASL:LII) gives something of his mood, as he looks back to his home shires from London. It was written circa 1891-2:

Here I lie down in London
And turn to rest alone.

There, by the starlit fences,
The wanderer halts and hears
My soul that lingers sighing
About the glimmering weirs.

Another poem that evokes this mood and time, though written a little later, is "As through the wild green hills of Wyre" (ASL:XXXVII), written August/September 1895:

You and I must keep from shame
In London streets the Shropshire name;
On banks of Thames they must not say
Severn breeds worse men than they ...
And if my foot returns no more
To Teme nor Corve nor Severn shore,

Luck, my lads, be with you still
By falling stream and standing hill ...

All through these years he kept on his shelf a picture of the St John's College boat crew, in which Moses Jackson was standing on the left. Throughout this period, Housman was using his restricted free time in preparing his brilliant and scrupulous classical papers. So successful was he in this, and such were his gifts and their application, that in 1892, after a decade of hard, lonely grind, he obtained the post of Latin Professor at University College, London. He did not fail to mention that he had failed to get a First at Oxford, but was able to attach testimonials from some seventeen scholars of eminence, including one from Germany and one from the United States. It was only a year or two after this, with his position so much more secure and agreeable, that his poetry started to trickle again into his notebooks.[1,2] In Housman's case it could rarely be said to "flow" but it was about to have one of its rare spates. There were several personal reasons for this, perhaps. His father died on 27th November 1894. Robert Louis Stevenson died in the same year and Housman submitted some unsigned verses to *The Academy* in tribute (AP:XXII). In 1889 Moses Jackson had married a widow, Mrs Rosa Chambers, and had taken her back to India where he was now Principal of Sind College, Karachi, where we may imagine him as a figure rather like Fielding in Forster's *A Passage to India*. In the "Epithalamion" that Housman drafted in 1889 but didn't finish or, certainly, publish till it came out as No. XXIV in *Last Poems*, in 1922, the year of Jackson's death, he writes:

So the groomsman quits your side
And the bridegroom seeks the bride:
Friend and comrade yield you o'er
To her that hardly loves you more.

In 1892 Jackson's brother Adalbert had died of typhoid, so by the end of 1894, by which time he was thirty-five, his mother and father and two closest friends had been taken from him. And the friend who meant most was in India, hence Housman's evocative use of the sub-continent's place names, perhaps. It was, with his failure to get a First, a bout of misfortune that could read like a Hardy novel. It is true he had secured his London Chair by now, but it perhaps explains why W S Blunt could say: "He would, I think, be quite silent if he were allowed to be," and Robert Bridges could exclaim: "Can you get him to talk? I can't." Even his sympathetic friend Percy Withers writes: "The choice lay between bleak silences and a constantly renewed effort to find subjects that would draw something more than a chilling and briefest possible comment."[3] At such times he may have felt accidie, or nothing, yet his poetry may have been in gestation, perhaps.

Whatever the cause the 1890s saw him jotting in his notebooks a good deal;

a process that came to particular consummation in the Spring and Summer of 1895 when we find him drafting or reworking so much of the material that became *A Shropshire Lad* (1896), though twenty or so pieces had been drafted earlier. The first five months of 1895 saw no less than twenty-three poems drafted, most of them being brought to their final state.[4] Another ten date from the month of August, though two or three of that list are reworkings. Lyrics written in the Spring of 1895 include "When I watch the living meet", "To an Athlete Dying Young", "1887" (second draft), "Oh see how thick the goldcup flowers", "Is my team ploughing?", and "Loveliest of trees". August saw poems such as "When smoke stood up from Ludlow", "As through the wild green hills of Wyre", and a further working of "Is my team ploughing?" (ASL:XXVII):

> I cheer a dead man's sweetheart,
> Never ask me whose.

He himself has spoken of how they came to be written in those months in the mid-1890s that he found so poetically charged.[5] He says that as he took his afternoon walks on Hampstead Heath, he found that lines and verses came to him, which he would write out when he got home, and complete, painfully, over a prolonged period at times, as his notebooks show. It was reminiscent of Keats in 1819, his "marvellous year", this productive period that produced not only so much of *A Shropshire Lad* but some work that appeared either in *Last Poems* or was published posthumously. He says that he was in a state of continuous excitement, arising, as it seemed to him, from the "pit of the stomach". Once, twice, in an afternoon, the spring might bubble up. He describes it as something of a torment and labour, yet one would be surprised if he did not derive *some* pleasure from the original creative impulse, or from the inevitable few minutes absorption and self-forgetfulness involved, if not from the revision process which seems to have been particularly arduous for him. It may have been an academic pose, this denial of the possibility of composition being enjoyable. Equally it may have been a pose to imply that he was a mere vehicle of the Muse, for the whole conception may have been an elaborate artifice, conceived in cold blood in the brain of the Professor of Latin; yet it would be hard to say, even in that case, that it was not inspired. As for the afflatus, the rush of ideas - usually when one is shaving - is not so unusual. There *are* fecund months or days; propitious moments, often in early morning or late in the evening, and one has to make the most of them.

The poem "Loveliest of trees, the cherry now" is almost cheerful;[6] Housman must have had a good lunch that day, perhaps. "1887" illustrates that there is as much taking thought as afflatus in fact, as it dates from 1895 and not from the Jubilee year[7] and took shape over a period. It illustrates, too, his thumping rhymes and rhythms, and the typical zest of his alliteration:

Oh, God will save her, fear you not:
Be you the men you've *been*,
Get you the sons your fathers *got*,
And *God* will save the *Queen*.

What were his models for these poems? Theirs is a distinctive voice, yet it sounds traditional notes, quite deliberately, and so is bound to have affinities. The Bible, Shakespeare, and Heine were influences. There is an obvious kinship with Hardy. Less obvious are his classical sources. Arnold and Browning he admired, and there are poems here and there that show traces of Swinburne. Kipling he appreciated, as well as Stevenson, and the Border ballads share his popular appeal and down-to-earth manner. Arnold he particularly admired, both as poet and critic. Writing of him as critic, he said:

> I go to Mr Leslie Stephen, and I am always instructed, though I may not be charmed. I go to Mr Walter Pater, and I am always charmed, though I may not be instructed. But Arnold was not merely instructive or charming nor both together: he was what it seems to me no one else is: he was illuminating.[8]

Note the characteristic distinction there that Housman gives to his prose. As to the effect of Arnold's poetry on Housman, who wrote this?

> Creep into thy narrow bed,
> Creep, and let no more be said!
> Vain thy onset! all stands fast.
> Thou thyself must break at last.

That, of course, is from Arnold's "The Last Word" (1867), which ends:

> Let the victors, when they come,
> When the forts of folly fall,
> Find thy body by the wall!

Similarities of mood and metre are evident, if coincidental; in the posthumously published *More Poems* of 1936, we find:

> O youth that will attain,
> On, for thine hour is short.
> It may be thou shalt gain
> The hell defended fort.

It is fair to remind ourselves that he did not publish that in his lifetime, and that his best poems transcend such stock images, but there are notes sounded that occur throughout his work.

The first edition of *A Shropshire Lad* was published at the author's expense, at a cost of £30.

In 1911 Housman was appointed Kennedy Professor of Latin at Cambridge and became a Fellow of Trinity. There he remained, continuing to keep himself to himself for the most part, but living relatively contentedly.

In 1922, the year Moses Jackson died, is a significant year in literature. It is the year of Joyce's *Ulysses* and Eliot's *Waste Land*; of Mansfield's *Garden*

Party and Edith Sitwell's *Façade* and Virginia Woolf's *Jacob's Room*. Yet it is also the year of Hardy's *Late Lyrics* and Housman's *Last Poems*. There may not be so many things that are quite so well known in this collection, as in *A Shropshire Lad*, but it contains some of his most moving, beautifully-worked poems such as "In valleys green and still" (LP:VII). The extraordinary thing is that the last verse of that poem was first drafted in April/May 1895, at the height of the spate that produced so much of *A Shropshire Lad*; the line before it ("And both are sighing") was produced some time between 1902 and 1905, and the remaining fifteen lines were not set down till April 1922, when the new collection was nearly ready for publication. Housman originally wrote the concluding stanza in this form:

> And you with colours gay
> And martial music swelling
> Walk the resounding way
> To the still dwelling.

In the final version, the first two lines now read:

> And down the distance they
> With dying note and swelling ...[9]

– with alliterative, sound and rhythmic improvement, and the evocation of a well-known phenomenon in the second line; immense gain, in fact, even if the individual detail of the "colours" has had to be lost. It is a good indication of the way he kept his work by him, and weighed every phrase. In this regard his discrimination in leaving so much of his work to be published posthumously - he himself being uncertain that it was up to the standard of his best - underlines his artistic tact. The concluding three poems of *Last Poems* are among his best. The first of the three is one of the most haunting (LP:XXXIX):

> When summer's end is nighing
> And skies at evening cloud,
> I muse on change and fortune
> And all the feats I vowed
> When I was young and proud.

So the first verse. In the fifth he reminds us that, in his earlier days, things might go badly, the day be "cloudy" at its "close":

> But air of other summers
> Breathed from beyond the snows,
> And I had hope of those.

– the thought and expression here are characteristic of what, over the years, has drawn certain readers to Housman, limited as his range and oeuvre may be. In the especially beautiful (LP:XL) we have already suggested the influence of Swinburne:

> Tell me not here, it needs not saying,
> What tune the enchantress plays

In aftermaths of soft September
Or under blanching mays ...

The closing words of "Fancy's Knell" (LP:XLI) fittingly end his book:

Come lads, and learn the dances
And praise the tune to-day.
To-morrow, more's the pity,
Away we both must hie,
To air the ditty,
And to earth I.

Again we find the archaisms (more or less) such as "nighing", "hie", "ditty", and the inversions that are present in Hardy, yet again the thing works. A simple emotion is expressed in plain, clear, direct, chiselled terms, the words and sounds and rhythms being carefully chosen in conjunction with images and proper names, to contribute to the overall, apparently artless effect. This and *A Shropshire Lad* were the only books of his poetry to be published in his lifetime.

In 1927 he edited *Nine Essays* by Arthur Platt (1860-1925) who had been his colleague at University College, London. The Preface which Housman contributed reveals a rarely seen tenderness, geniality even, of tone, occasioned doubtless by the fact that Platt was an unassuming, individual, and very kindly man. For some seventeen years, in fact, three outstanding men had been together at University College, Housman, Latin Professor, Platt, Greek Professor, and W P Ker, Professor of English Language and Literature. The historian of the College writes: "In Ker, Housman and Platt the college had a trio not exceeded by any group in its history in reputation or in its affections."[10] After mentioning Platt's scholarly achievements; his endearing intimacies with a leopard, a giraffe and a gnu at the London Zoo; his willingness to address the college literary society and his happy accord with his students; his marriage and his two children, his addition to tobacco and his habit of squandering "long summer days on watching the game of cricket", Housman concludes:

His happy and useful life is over, and now begins the steady encroachment of oblivion, as those who remember him are in their turn summoned away. This record will not preserve, perhaps none could preserve, more than an indistinct and lifeless image of the friend who is lost to us: good, kind, bright, unselfish, and as honest as the day; versatile without shallowness, accomplished without ostentation, a treasury of hidden knowledge which only accident brought to light, but which accident brought to light perpetually, and which astonished us so often that astonishment lost its nature and we should have wondered more if wonders had failed. Yet what most eludes description is not the excellence of his gifts but the singularity of his essential being, his utter unlikeness to any other creature in the world.

Thus his geniality in 1927. The following year saw the death of Hardy. Housman agreed to be a pallbearer but showed the other side of his nature by nearly withdrawing when he heard that Galsworthy had been invited too. He refused various doctorates – and the Order of Merit, in terms which were uncertainly tactful - but in 1911 he had accepted an honorary Fellowship at his old college, St John's. He did not smoke but took an interest in food and wine. He read Proust and detective stories in those last years when ill health added to his temperamental morosity. He lectured till very near the end of his life, making play with a window pole, shuffling his notes, and breaking the silence at punctually five minutes past the hour, and occasionally, as Enoch Powell has related, reading a favourite passage with tears in his eyes. He died on 30th April 1936, his ashes being laid under the North wall of the parish church in Ludlow. A tablet bears the first phrases from "Parta Quies" (MP:XLVIII):

> Good-night; ensured release,
> Imperishable peace ...

It is the last poem of *More Poems*[11], the posthumous collection garnered and published by his younger brother Laurence Housman (1865-1959)[12], in the year A.E.H. died. The penultimate poem of the collection (MP:XLVII): "O thou that from thy mansion", is actually entitled "For my funeral"; it has a tone akin to Swinburne, Kipling's "Recessional", and many a hymn. "I to my perils" (MP:VI) is delightfully Hardy-esque in theme, and song-like in the extreme. In the following year Laurence published a memoir with further poems,[13] eighteen of which, together with four or five others, found their way into the *Collected Poems* as *Additional Poems*,[14] The poet's characteristic brevity is maintained; several are quatrains only. Included is the tribute to R.L.S. and (AP:VI) with its telling line: "Ask me no more, for fear I should reply." It is pleasant to close this essay not in the "fervour of gloom", however, but with a reference to his little-known humorous verse. Housman's parody of "The shades of night were falling fast" is certainly worth reading, as is his "Fragment of an English opera" which begins:

> Retire, my daughter;
> Prayers have been said;
> Take your warm water
> And go to bed ...

– or the somewhat Milne- or Belloc-like fun of "Aunts and Nieces":

> Some nieces won't, some nieces can't
> Imbibe instruction from an aunt ...[15]

It is not of this, however, but of hills and places and of teams ploughing, and lads "in their hundreds to Ludlow come in for the fair", and of "the old wind in the old anger", that we think when we think of him.[16, 17]

Notes
1 *The Collected Poems of A E Housman*. Cape, 1934 (1948, etc)
2 *The Manuscript Poems of A E Housman*; edited by T B Haber, OUP, 1955 (A fascinating study of material from four of Housman's notebooks)
3 Withers, P. *A Buried Life*, 1940
4 Ref.2, 13-21 (14)

5 Cf. Housman, A.E. *The Name and Nature of Poetry*. (lecture). Cambridge, 1933
6 Certainly the Bible Class leader must have thought so who gave the author a pocket edition in 1949 and pointed out that poem. It is hard to realise that Housman had been dead only thirteen years.
7 See Appendix II: Pearce, B.L. "Jubilee Verses: some poems written for Q. Victoria's 1887 Jubilee." *Journal RSA*, CXXV (5372), July 1987, 573-4
8 Closing words of an informal London University lecture on Arnold.
9 See Ref.2, 22-23
10 Bellot, H Hale. *University College London 1826-1926*, 1929, 388 (a later alumnus may be excused pleasure in the closing words of the sentence)
11 No sign of "catch-titles" here. Alice Meynell would have approved but one's sympathy is increased for the genre.
12 Laurence Housman, pacifist and feminist sympathiser, was the author of *The Little Plays of St Francis* (1922) and *Victoria Regina* (1937). He edited his brother's *More Poems* (1936) and compiled *AEH* ... (1937), for which see Ref.13.
13 Housman, L. *A.E.H.; Some Poems, etc.*, 1937 (includes a memoir)
14 As John Carter explains in a "Note on the Text" in the *Collected Poems* (Ref. 1, above)
15 All to be found in Housman, A.E. *Collected Poems and Prose*; edited by Christopher Ricks. Allen Lane/Penguin Press, 1988 (235, 245-6, 251-2) A comprehensive, excellently presented collection.
16 (ASL:XXIII & XXXI)
17 Based on lectures given at the National Portrait Gallery on 8th July 1992 and 8th September 1993.

17. MASEFIELD: YEATS: & THE DRAMA

1. Masefield was an admirer of Housman. In his *Letters to Reyna* (1983), he quotes Housman's epitaph on the Salvation Army's .... Colonel Mary Jane:

'Halle-lu-jah' was the only exclamation
That escaped Lieutenant-Colonel Mary Jane
When she fell from off the platform at the Station
And was cut to little pieces by the train ...[1]

In the same letter of 1956 he writes:

I love you to love A E Housman, for I have loved him dearly for 58 years now: & tho I did not often see him, I admired him deeply. (Hardy was of the 19th cent. & earlier.) AEH was a very fine fellow, but I never heard of his fiddling (nor, in spite of his noble poem about Abdon Burf)[2] of his fifing: but he may have done both. (Hardy was both a singer and a musician; I think he cd play fiddle, flute, piano & serpent; & he knew an infinity of songs and hymns.)[3, 4]

In 1963 he writes again, regarding Housman's poems:

... they came, away back, just at the very time when they could be all the world to me: and for years they were. I have his poems on the table always, and as Ben Jonson said of WS 'I loved the man ... on this side idolatry.' [5]

Later the same year he refers to "On Wenlock Edge" (ASL:XXXI) and to the line: "When Uricon the city stood":

Did you ever go to Uricon? There is a vast heap of basilica or forum wall in the midst of grass. The forum must once have been just about the measure of Birmingham Town Hall; & the city about a mile across; & the lovely brook once its drink and bath now romping free to the Severn.[6]

2. Masefield as a young man came upon W B Yeats' *Poems* of 1899 and, shy as he was, was determined to make the older poet's acquaintance.[7] In the autumn of 1900 he was invited to Yeats' lodgings at 18 Woburn Buildings (now 5 Woburn Walk) in Bloomsbury, where Yeats lived from 1895 - 1919, his friends at this period including T Sturge Moore, Brooke, Symons, Pound, Tagore, Eliot and Binyon, Robert Bridges; the artists William Rothenstein and Shannon and Ricketts. Yeats and Binyon were kind to him and encouraged him.

In his *Some Memories of W B Yeats* (1940) he has described Yeats' rooms:

There were also these things: Blake's first Dante engraving, *The Whirlwind of lovers*; a little engraving of Blake's head; a print of Blake's *Ancient of Days*; and a little engraving from the *Job*. ... The chairs were dark; the effect of the room was sombre. ... After 1904-7, he added to the room a big, dark blue lectern, on which his Kelmscott Chaucer stood, between enormous candles in big blue sconces. ... On Monday evenings, from eight until two or three in the morning, he was at home to his friends. ...[8]

In 1966 he wrote about this to "Reyna":

Usually 1 or 2 ... would dine with WBY at about 6.45 before the Evening began about 8 p.m. These in all made about 20 more, whom I never knew well: and those whom I did know, alas ... I think they are all gone into the world of light, I alone sit sorrowing here.[9]

Masefield was one who carved his initials on the copper beech at Coole, Yeats, AE, Shaw, Synge and Augustus John being amongst the others. With Jack Yeats, the poet's painter brother, he used to make model ships and later, when Yeats was convalescing at Rapallo in 1930, he visited him and undertook to build him a model brigantine, which was duly delivered.[10] From 1919 they could meet again, when Yeats moved to Oxford,[11] and in 1935 Masefield visited Yeats in Ireland on his birthday. In 1936 Yeats' edition of *The Oxford Book of Modern Verse* appeared. Of Masefield's poems, Yeats included "Sea-Change", "Port of Many Ships", "A Valediction (Liverpool Docks)", "Trade Winds", "Port of Holy Peter", and the much anthologised "Cargoes."

3. About 1903 Masefield and Gordon Bottomley were associated with Yeats in attempts to revive the poetic drama. Yeats was seeking to realise his vision of a "Theatre of Beauty," and the short-lived society "The Masquers" was founded at this time by Yeats, Gilbert Murray, and T Sturge Moore, amongst others.[12, 13] A further impetus was given to poetic drama by George Bell's initiative in seeking to present Christian plays in Canterbury Cathedral.[14] It was due to him that Masefield's *The Coming of Christ* (1928), and the plays of Eliot and Fry were to be given there. Bottomley's *The Acts of St Peter* (1933) was put on at Exeter Cathedral. Bottomley was a pioneer in the movement toward a more colloquial engagement; a Yorkshireman with Pre-Raphaelite leanings.[15] It was an idealist, yet practical movement which has enriched our literature, as a result of which the plays of T S Eliot and the rich, human oeuvre of Christopher Fry reached the London commercial stage as well as the nave or chancel.[16, 17, 18] In this Yeats and Masefield were pioneers. Masefield, who was to present plays at his Boar's Hill home near Oxford, had already written *The Tragedy of Man* (1909), and *The Trial of Jesus* (1925), besides *The Coming of Christ*, and a number of other plays. Another aspect of Masefield's interest - and one that remained with him throughout his life, once he had discovered Malory - was the amount of work he produced on Arthurian themes. This included, besides much poetry, *Tristan and Isolt: a play in verse*[19, 20] and the unpublished *When Good King Arthur* which Dodd dates to circa 1919-32 - "and almost surely after 1922, when he became so interested in the speaking of poetry."[21] another link with Yeats, as it happens.

As to Yeats' "theatre", how is one to categorise plays so many and various, except that they ceaselessly experiment; ceaselessly seek to communicate; to speak to a contemporary audience, and to adapt accordingly; are always "poetic" and "ideal" in mood, and are usually intended for a discerning audience in a "chamber" theatre - though his plays for the Abbey Theatre go far to invalidate this generalisation. There are his "national" plays – *The Countess Cathleen, The Land of Heart's Desire* and the Cuchulain cycle, moving as in

On Baile's Strand, moving and humorous, as in *The Green Helmet;* his *Deirde*, a theme which Synge also treated. There is the influence of the Noh plays of Japan in *At the Hawk's Well, The Only Jealousy of Emer, The Death of Cuchulain*, and *Purgatory*, that spare, late play, in which he threw off the enthralment to blank verse and the Elizabethans which so haunted the Victorian and Edwardian poet-dramatists, and produced a shortened, *spoken* line which achieves the effects Eliot aimed at in an intense, and different, manner:

> ... Study that tree
> It stands there like a purified soul,
> All cold, sweet, glistening light.
> ...
> And she must animate that dead night
> Not once but many times ...[22]

There is the early Romantic aspiration of *The Shadowy Waters*; his versions of *Oedipus Rex* and *Oedipus at Colonus*, and his unique, poignant evocation of Jonathan Swift in the prose of *The Words upon the Window Pane*.[23,24] Between this basically 20th century oeuvre, and Shelley's *Cenci*, there is not too much to set against the comment:

> It is strange to reflect that (W.S.) Gilbert is the only writer to use verse with complete success in the Victorian theatre. It is true that his range was confined to the comic, ironic and sentimental, and would have been scorned by poets whose ambitions lay in historical tragedy. Yet he knew his theatre; they did not show that they knew theirs.[25]

Notes
1 John Masefield: *Letters to Reyna*, edited by William Buchan. Buchan & Enright, 1983, Letter 142, page 142
2 Housman's "Fancy's Knell" (*Last Poems*: XLI)
3 Cf. Ref. 1
4 Masefield admired Hardy also, and referred to him as "the Master". Cf. Ref. 1, Letter 561, page 456
5. Letter 441, page 373
6 Letter 446, page 377
7 William Buchan, Ref. 1, 18
8 Quoted in A N Jeffares' *W B Yeats: a new biography*. Arena, 1990. 144-5; see also chapter 2, above, Ref.4
9 Ref. 1, Letter 161, page 491
10 Joseph Hone: *W B Yeats 1965-1939*. Macmillan, 1942, 138, 181, 412 (etc.)
11 Ref. 8, 203
12 Ref. 10, 189-192
13 Cf. eg. Yeats, W.B. "The Theatre" in *Ideas of Good and Evil*. A H Bullen, 1903, 257-269
14 It parallels his initiative which resulted in the "Bloomsbury" painters creating the murals to be seem in Bewick church, near Lewes.
15 E Martin Browne *Verse in the Modern English Theatre*. Cardiff, University of Wales Press. 1963, 8-10, eg.
16 Trewin, J C *Verse Drama since 1800*. Cambridge, National Book League, 1956
17 Peacock, R *The Poet in the Theatre*. Macgibbon & Kee, 1961
18 Pearce B.L. "The Poet in the Theatre: Poet's View". *Message 66* (Paris), Autumn 1966,

12-15

19 Masefield, John *John Masefield*; edited and introduced by D L Dodds (in the Arthurian Poets series). Woodbridge, Boydell Press, 1994, 198-261

20 Crocker Wight. *John Masefield* ... (a bibliography). Boston (USA), The Boston Athenaeum, 1992, 116-118

21 Ref. 19, 21, 288-330

22 Yeats. W B *The Collected Plays.* 2nd edition. Macmillan, 1952 (1953), 688-9

23 Ure, P. *Yeats the Playwright.* Routledge & Kegan Paul, 1963

24 Bushrui, S B *Yeats' Verse Plays: The Revisions 1900-1910.* Oxford, 1965

25 Price, C J L "The Victorian Theatre" in *The Victorians*; edited by Arthur Pollard. Sphere, 1969 (1970), 393

18. MASEFIELD

John Masefield (1878-1967) poet laureate, was born at The Knapp, Ledbury, Herefordshire, within sight of the Malvern Hills (home to "Piers Plowman") on the 1st June 1878. He was thus a Gemini, a happy star sign for poets[1] which he shared with Hardy and Yeats - and with Elgar who was born a few miles away in Worcestershire. Ledbury remains a pleasant country town, with a station on the railway line between Hereford and Malvern, and has associations with Elizabeth Barrett Browning as well as with Masefield. The poet's father was George Edward Masefield, a solicitor;[2] his mother Caroline Louisa (née Barker). The Masefields retain a strong connection in the area as family solicitors, and The Knapp is now the home of W H Masefield, the current head of the family. In 1885, when the boy was six and a half years of age, his mother died of bronchitis and double pneumonia, a few weeks after giving birth to her sixth child. He came to wonder in later life whether an accident she had when a carriage was upset at a hunt meeting had anything to do with her death. Their nurse, Maymie, had to leave to take care of her own mother, so the children were doubly bereft. A brisk governess by the name of Mrs Broers was put in charge of them, and the unpleasant and sinister governess in *The Midnight Folk* is doubtlessly inspired by her. Such a caricature may have been undeserved, but Masefield certainly found her unsympathetic - and in his own words "vulgar" - and she was clearly no substitute for the lost mother or nurse. In March 1886 his grandfather died, and the family finances were found to be far from healthy. His grandfather had lived at The Priory, close to the (Ledbury) Parish Church. His other grandfather had been rector of Great Comberton, under Bredon Hill (shades of Housman): he died when John was five, but until then the boy used to be taken on visits there. But now the family was moved from The Knapp to The Priory. Alas, the dreaded Mrs Broers went with them, and John had to leave behind the honey-suckled garden of The Knapp in which he had delighted. But The Priory had its own enchantments. His later description of it reminds one of the early experiences of C S Lewis:

> It was a rambling pretty house in a great garden ... a very, very old house, full of passages, corridors, strange rooms, strange noises .. and a strange, dark uncanny place, with rooms never opened, and cupboards and secret chambers.

It anticipates *The Midnight Folk* and Kay's adventures in that book, as well as the beginnings of some of Lewis's "Narnia" stories, writing, as he was, a lot later than Masefield. The other great enrichment was his grandfather's library, in which he could find a good deal of exciting fiction, which he would slip away to read under a bed in a spare room, so that he could enjoy it in peace. This supplemented the history, French, geography and "three Rs", which Mrs Broers imparted. Tranquillity and unease contended in him, however. Not only had he lost his mother, and his early imaginary world at The Knapp, of which she was a part; he believed himself damned and destined for hell and, by bad fortune, his place in church was opposite a stone pillar on which was carved the face of a tortured sinner. He could, however, look forward to occasional visits to Woollas Hall, on the slopes of Bredon Hill, where his godmother, Ann Hanford-Flood, lived - a former friend of his mother's, who wanted to do her best for him. There, till he was thirteen, he could find another old house, another library, and Ann's kindness. In January 1888, when he was nine and a half, he became a boarder at Warwick School; was very unhappy at first, and in the Spring began to write his first few scribbles of poetry - always a sign of the direst misery - but became happier in 1889, when a Junior House was opened. He made friends easily and took part in the sporting life of the school. But in 1891, when he was still only thirteen, his father died at the early age of 49. Uncle William and Aunt Kate took over The Priory and with it the children's management. He was taken away from the school[3] and given another governess at The Priory. Aunt Kate's sense of duty exceeded her capacity to inspire love in her young nephews and nieces, as Constance Babington Smith puts it in her admirable biography, and one of her worst deeds, in John Masefield's eyes, was to get rid of his grandfather's books. It was John himself that they "got rid" of next, for it was decided that he should be trained for a life at sea - by no means his own choice though, like so many of us, he was not certain at that early stage what he *did* want to do. He was reconciled to his lot, however, through the kindness of a temporary governess, a Miss Barnsdale, whose brother had been in the training ship for which he was destined. So it was that in the autumn of 1891, still only thirteen, he joined HMS *Conway*, moored in the Mersey, and began to acquire that knowledge of the sea and a seaman's life that informs *Dauber* (his narrative poem of 1913) and so many of his ballads. He found the life difficult at first, with its need to distinguish between "yow, yow" / "yow, YOW" / or "YOW, yow-yow", each giving a different instruction, but he soon learnt to row and dive, polish, sweep, and make up hammocks, besides pursuing ordinary lessons and getting some idea of navigation and astronomy. The basic training was still in sail though the transition to steam was well under way. By the second year he was happy enough, and in his final summer won a telescope for a prize essay demonstrating efficiency in "Writing, Spelling and Composition". It was his habit to calm himself for sleep by reciting poetry in his head, as he lay in his hammock.[4] His mathematics was not his strong point, so he stayed on for a few extra months and left the *Conway* with his seamanship certificate in March 1894. He was still a little short of sixteen.

In April 1894 he sailed from Cardiff for Cape Horn and Iquique (Chile) on the *Gilcruix*, a four-masted barque. The battles with the "River Plate squalls", when they reached the South Atlantic, were to find their way into *Dauber*:

He caught one giddy glimpsing of the deck
Filled with white water, as though heaped with snow ...

– though the poem would not be written for some years, when he had read Chaucer and the Romantics with all their narrative command and alliterative and metric power; for the present, he kept a journal. He was not always well, but seems to have been able to play his part, even to the notorious wrestling with the rigging in a fierce gale, and (or so his journal would have us believe) to have enjoyed it, but he was still only sixteen. The Captain was kindly and when Masefield fell ill at Iquique with sunstroke (and perhaps with nervous prostration) he arranged with the British Consul for him to be sent home by steamship as a "Distressed British Seaman." After a period in hospital at Valparaiso, he returned home via Panama, his passing through the Caribbean doubtless giving him inspiration for the ballads and passages in his stories that were to come. He was back in Ledbury by the end of October, 1894, having had enough of the sea, and knowing now that he wanted to be a writer. But Aunt Kate insisted that he seek another berth and by the following Spring he had obtained a place on the *Bidston Hill*, another four-masted barque, which he was to join at New York. When he got to New York, however, in March 1895, he made himself scarce, though with only a pound or two in his pocket, and did not join his ship. William Masefield resorted to private detectives to trace him, but without success. Now penniless, and not quite seventeen, he was to acquire his lifelong sympathy with the drifter, the unfortunate, the persecuted and the weak. He cut wood and helped out on farms; got a job in a bar in Greenwich Village, then got taken on at a carpet factory in Yonkers. The job was menial, easily mastered, and boring. But he found a bookshop and Malory - which set him off on his lifelong interest in Arthurian legend[5] - discovered Keats, Shelley and Chaucer, and saved up to buy their poetry, and was led to turn to Peacock, Rossetti and Morris. Masefield was creating for himself a rich private world of self-cultivation, in fact, in despite of his surroundings; exactly what John Cowper Powys, also an American wanderer (as lecturer) for much of his life, was to advocate in his illuminating manner.[6] Masefield himself quotes the Buddha: "... dwell as having refuge in yourselves, resorts in yourselves, and not elsewhere." In this way it may be possible to preserve our souls, our real selves, amid humdrum labours or alien circumstance. Shakespeare and Milton were other poets he turned to, and by December 1896, when he was eighteen, he was writing some sonnets. His lot was not easy, nor did it offer any hopeful path toward a better future. Having given his guardian so much trouble, by not taking up his berth in the *Bidston Hill* and going to ground without sending any word to him, he did not feel that he could now approach him for financial help. A friend did so on his behalf but received a stern rebuff. This might seem hard, but we have to consider the cost and trouble his guardian had been put to, and that he had a duty to the poet's brothers and sisters as well as to him. The young man knew that if he was to do anything he would have to do it himself. He decided that London was the place to be in, if he was to be a writer, and managed to work his passage back on a steamer bound for Liverpool. He arrived back in England in July 1897, just nineteen, with six pounds and a revolver. Whilst failing to get a job in Liverpool he fed his mind on the paintings in the Walker Art Gallery. His sister Ethel found him a job as a junior clerk in a London office, where he coped as best as he could, in poor physical condition, and lodged in the cheapest rooms he could find, much as W E Henley had done at a similar juncture. He suffered from malaria, "trances and night-sweats" and depression brought on by quinine. His situation was eased slightly when an Uncle on his mother's side, John Parker, a London solicitor, persuaded William Masefield to advance him a little of his father's money to help him regain his health. Within a few weeks he was working as a clerk in the Capital and Counties Bank in London. The work was demanding. It brought him barely enough to live on, but there he stayed for some three years, from early 1898 to 1901. In June 1899, *The Outlook* published one of his sea-poems, later re-titled "The Turn of the Tide." He came into touch again with Miss (Ann) Flood, his godmother, now in her late forties. He corresponded enthusiastically. They met as well as wrote, and she was of great help to him. These were happier developments but the happiest was the result of his pleasure in W B Yeats' *Poems* of 1899. Yeats often spent his winters in London and in the autumn of 1900 Masefield approached him and got himself invited to 18 Woburn Buildings, on Guy Fawkes night. Mrs Old, Yeats' housekeeper, opened the door and showed his upstairs to the living room.[7] Yeats was friendly and encouraging, being himself in his mid-thirties. In due course he introduced Masefield to Lady Gregory, Laurence Binyon, William Strang - who was to do an etching of him in 1912 - William Rotherstein and John Synge, besides many other artists and writers, and later would include several of Masefield's sea ballads in his *Oxford Book of Modern Verse*. In the summer of 1901 Masefield moved from Walthamstow to Barton Street, where he was near Binyon who was in Smith Square, and came to the momentous decision to give up his job, momentous for someone so little established in literature or financial resources. At times his prospects and spirits were at a low ebb, but they could resurge, and somehow he managed to keep going, principally by journalism or editorial work. Soon he moved to 15 Coram Street to be near Yeats in Bloomsbury. In 1902 his first book *Saltwater Ballads* came out from Grant Richards[8] and the immortal "Sea Fever", was amongst them, the first line then beginning, "I must down to the sea again", without the subsequent "go" after the "must"; a second book, *Ballads* appeared the following year. "Cargoes" and the lovely "Trade Winds" illustrate his lyric concision at its best, whilst there are fuller poems and ballads in which the youthful poet exults in his colloquial and narrative powers. He himself mentions Keats and Chaucer and the songs of Shakespeare, as among his influences and inspirations. Kipling, born the same year as Yeats, was to some extent working in parallel. It is a tribute to the quality and popularity of these poems that so many have been set to music, and that so often we still hear them sung. They have a lilt and music of their own - nowhere more so than in "Captain Stratton's Fancy", the title itself assonant, where "some are fond of fiddles, and a song well sung" - yet not in such a way as to preclude setting in a traditional manner, for they have regularity, and use refrain and repetition tellingly. They were written, of course, at a time when the drawing-room or "art" ditty was somewhat more in vogue, and when Britain was still very much a sea-faring nation, and proud of it. There is John Ireland's well-known setting of "Sea Fever". Ireland himself is said to have become chagrined that this song was so popular at the expense, as he saw it, of his other work. Yet the song's success is in part a tribute to the evocative, heartfelt directness of Masefield's poem. The same may be said in the case of the rollicking swing Peter Warlock (Philip Heseltine) gives to "Captain Stratton's Fancy" or the gentle rocking mood of Frederick Keel's setting of "Trade Winds." Keel (1871-1950) was a baritone and teacher, as well as a composer; secretary of the Folk Song Society 1911-19, and editor of its journal.[9]

In 1901, when in his twenty-third year, Masefield met Constance Crommelin, a thirty-five old teacher who had read mathematics at Newnham, Cambridge,[10] and had stayed on for a fourth year to read classics and English literature. She was on terms of close friendship with Isabel Fry, sister of Roger Fry the painter and critic, and Margery Fry, librarian, later Principal, of Somerville College. When Masefield and Constance married in 1903, the latter continued to extend the closest friendship to Isabel, whilst doing much for Masefield's personal and cultural development. It was in 1903 that he met John Synge,[11] and this, though Synge wrote in prose, was a further spur to produce poetic drama.[12] In 1904-5 he visited Lady Gregory at Coole Park. He became friendly with Yeats' brother, J B (Jack) Yeats, the painter, and his wife, and when Masefield's *A Mainsail Haul* (stories) came out in 1905, Jack contributed a frontispiece. He and Constance lived in Marylebone Road; then in Greenwich, then in "Little Venice", but in 1912 moved to 13 Well Walk, Hampstead, a road that has connections with Keats, Constable, and Thomas Sturge Moore. His play *The Tragedy of Nan* appeared in 1909, and now his narrative poems began to come out, too: *The Everlasting Mercy* in 1911; *The Widow in the Bye Street*, in 1912, and *Dauber* in 1913, the protagonist of *Dauber* being an artist, in part an "objective correlative" for himself, shown experiencing the rough sea life and manners that he himself encountered in his voyage round the Horn. It is to his credit that he produced so much creative work whilst, at this period, being of necessity involved in an immense amount of day to day journalism. 1910 saw his *Ballads and Poems* and *The Tragedy of Pompey the Great.* The plays he produced in his early and mid-career owed much to Yeats and Synge, and the encouragement of the former, as well as to Arthurian sources and Shakespeare. He was encouraged also by Granville Barker, Gilbert Murray, and George Bell, later Bishop of Chichester.[13] Lillah McCarthy appeared at the Haymarket in the title role of "Nan".

Following the birth of his son Lewis, there came a brief infatuation with the American author and actress Elizabeth Robins (again a lady older than himself) at a time when he was excessively overworked, but the lady tactfully disengaged herself. It was at this time that he wrote the deeply felt poem to his mother entitled simply "CLM", with the energy and phrasing that Housman would have admired:

In the dark womb where I began
My mother's life made me a man.
Through all the months of human birth
Her beauty fed my common earth.
I cannot see, nor breathe, nor stir,
But through the death of some of her.

Down in the darkness of the grave
She cannot see the life she gave.
For all her love, she cannot tell
Whether I use it ill or well,
Nor knock at dusty doors to find
Her beauty dusty in the mind.[14]

– and his commitment to the woman's movement, exemplified by the speech he made in the Queen's Hall in 1910,[15] given such fervent expression in verses 4 and 5:

What have I done to keep in mind
My debt to her and womankind?
...
What have I done, or tried, or said
In thanks to that dear woman dead?
Men triumph over women still,
Men trample women's rights at will ...

The popularity of his narrative poems created a certain jealousy amongst writers such as Rupert Brooke, who one would have supposed to have had status and following enough. and from J C Squire there came parodies of his style which were not all that kindly intentioned. In June 1913 the poet laureate Alfred Austin died and there was speculation as to his successor. Squire suggested Masefield, with heavy irony that misfired and was taken as serious commendation. Masefield had no illusions. He considered himself too young, too rebellious, and too coarse for the job. He suggested six candidates, putting

Bridges first, and it was Bridges who was appointed - but his turn was to come. At the outbreak of the First World War, he and Constance had just taken Lollingdon Farm, near Wallingford, on the edge of the Berkshire Downs, and it was only now that they began to see less of Isabel Fry, which relieved certain tensions. It was there he wrote "August 1914":

> These homes, this valley spread below me here,
> The rooks, the tilted stacks, the beasts in pen,
> Have been the heartfelt things, past-speaking dear
> To unknown generations of dead men ...[16]

He wrote a number of sonnets at this time, too, which came out in 1916, as *Sonnets and Poems*. Soon he went out and worked for the Red Cross in France and the Dardanelles - at one time working with the artist Henry Tonks, Slade tutor of Gwen and Augustus John, who had gone out as a volunteer surgeon. He then undertook a lecture tour in America where, stiff and nervous as his delivery was, his genuineness won most audiences. One pleasant feature was that some of the people he had known when down on his luck in New York in the 1890s came to meet him. He was asked to return to France to write up the Battle of the Somme, but denied access to official records he was only able to produce a description of the battlefield, *The Old Front Line* (1917) and a later short book on the battle itself in 1919. He was then sent off to the States again, this time on a tour of a propaganda character. By the end of the War, Constance had moved the family from Lollingdon to Boars Hill, with its fine views over Oxford and the Berkshire Downs. Here he initiated verse-speaking competitions at Oxford and developed (or indulged) his lifelong interest in the theatre,[17] Over the next ten years he produced fine work in a variety of genres. In 1919 there appeared *Reynard the Fox*, that breathless narrative and evocation, full of rhyme and alliteration and a great deal of compassionate observation:

> Two hundred yards and the trees grew taller,
> Blacker, blinder, as hope grew smaller: ...
> He was all one ache, one gasp, one thirsting,
> Heart on his chest-bones, beating, bursting;
> The hounds were gaining like spotted pards,
> And the wood hedge was still a hundred yards.[18]

An equal insight into his spirit is to be found in the letter he wrote to his son Lewis when their cat had just died:[19]

> He drank some milk and licked at a sardine, and moved to a sheltered nest in the shrubbery, a favourite summer den of his, and passed the day there. In the evening when it was cooler ... I stayed some time with him, keeping off the flies ... I went out to him every half hour or so, with milk and so forth. He suffered no pain at all, of that I am certain, but I knew that he was dying ... At half past ten, I left him there at the brink of death; but I stroked him very gently and had from him something like the ghost of a purr. Very soon after this he turned a little ... and died very quietly from old age lying on his right side, as I have so often seen him asleep in the sun ... I put him in a box with flowers, grass, and lavender and buried him in his summer

haunt.

In 1925 came *The Trial of Jesus*, a passion play in three acts,[20] and in 1927 both *Tristan and Isolt*, his Arthurian play[21], and *The Midnight Folk*, one of his most enduring and popular works, with Kay, the young protagonist, and the governess who recalls his own. In this delightful and absorbing story, Masefield's invention anticipates Tolkien, C S Lewis, Alan Garner, and Barbara Sleigh's "Carbonnel" books, whether or not his work was a conscious inspiration to any of them.

"You are a wicked little boy, Kay", the governess said: "You will go straight to bed this minute, without your bread and milk."

The little boy went up to his room, in the old part of the house: there were oak beams in the ceiling; the floor was all oak plank. The bed was big and old, valanced to the floor, and topped by a canopy. Kay was very much afraid of it at going-to-bed time because so many tigers could get underneath it, to wait till he was asleep, but tonight he didn't mind ...

Now it became darker ... Footsteps passed in the house ... gleams of candlelight crossed the ceiling. Very strange creakings sounded ... there were scutterings to and fro, and scarping scratchings ...

There was Nibbins, the black cat.

"Come along, Kay", Nibbins said. "We can just do it while they're at the banquet; but don't make more noise than you must."

Kay peeped through the door. It opened from a little narrow passage in the thickness of the wall.

"Where does it lead to?" he asked.

"Come and see," Nibbins said ...[22]

In 1928 *The Coming of Christ* was published. For Masefield it marks the culmination if his long commitment to a poetic theatre, just as, in a wider context, it was a landmark in the revival of verse drama in Britain, based on Canterbury Cathedral[23]. It was performed in the Cathedral, in that year, to music by Gustav Holst, with costume design and production by Charles Ricketts, and was seen by more than 6,000 people, thus vindicating George Bell's vision in seeking to revive the idea of a Whitsuntide Mystery play, in line, as it happens, with the performances of Hofmannsthal's *Jedermann* in Salzburg this century. From this stemmed the work of Eliot, Christopher Fry, Charles Williams and others. Did Eliot have in mind a passage such as this, when he was thinking about the character and temptations of his Becket?:

King, priest and governor will turn against you,
Calling you rebel and blasphemer. Soon
Even the young will think you mad. Your followers
Will dwindle to a few, of whom some three
Will know the beauty of your thought.
You, knowing of your failure, will be tempted
To doubt your spirit's mission, and despair.
In agony, you will think that God forgets you. ...

To which comes the reply:

What torment cannot break, death cannot end:
He who endures even to the end is saved.[24]

In May 1930 he was appointed poet laureate, in succession to Robert Bridges, an appointment he held till his death in 1967. He pointed out that he was "not a ready writer" and could "write verse only rarely in moments of deep feeling." Ramsay MacDonald assured him that he need only write if the spirit moved him - but perhaps Masefield responded over the years to what he perceived as the call of duty more conscientiously than was necessary, and published more than was wise. It is illustrative of his innate sincerity and honesty, and the appointment went to one who could speak to the heart of a people. There are certain parallels, indeed - not to be taken too literally - with Thomas Hardy. In their elder days there is even some similarity in their case of feature; that slightly sad, reflective aspect, seen in certain photographs or pictures. They were both countrymen at heart. They were both compassionate, and natural seers. They both had a certain natural simplicity and dignity. They lived almost the same length of years and, in each case, the society and culture of the end of their lives was quite different from what it was at the start. They both lived honourable lives, and achieved industriously earned fame. They both drew inspiration from a number of women often but (especially in Masefield's earlier days) not always younger, a legacy from the early loss of his mother, perhaps. Some of these women they might have seen once in a lane; from others they drew an extended creative nourishment, enjoying a long responsive relationship, whether by letter or meeting or (in the case of Hardy) by recollection in the study, over long periods of their lives, to great creative effect. It was true for Elgar and for Janacek; for Yeats[25] and Patmore, confessedly, and for Browning, we may suspect. Masefield's appointment as laureate was widely approved. It was welcomed by Yeats and the normally aloof Housman. In 1935 he was to receive the Order of Merit, and other honours would follow. In April 1933 he and Constance rented a Cotswold manor house at Pinbury Park, where he wrote *A Box of Delights* (1935)[26] with its Kay again as protagonist, and its conflict between good and unpleasant people and influences. But the winters were cold at Pinbury, and Masefield felt increasingly at odds with the local hunting gentry. In 1938 they moved back near Oxford to Burcote Brook, a house just north of the Oxfordshire Dorchester. It burnt down soon after his death and the site became a Masefield Cheshire Home. But there Masefield was to live for nearly thirty years. A year after he moved in, there came the Second World War. In *The Nine Days Wonder* (1941) he wrote the story of the Dunkirk evacuation, whilst *Some Memories of W B Yeats* had appeared the previous year, in response to Yeats' death. Then in 1942 came the news that his son Lewis had died in North Africa as a result of artillery fire. Lewis had been a conscientious objector, and was serving in the R.A.M.C., much as his father had done in

122

World War I. It is sobering, too, that Masefield and Edward Thomas were born in the same year, the one dying in 1917 and the other fifty years later, and that Rupert Brooke, born nine years after them, and seemingly destined to lead a charmed life, died before either of them. His very fine poem "The Passing Strange" speaks, surely, to this condition:

> But in the darkest hour of night
> When even the foxes peer for sight,
> The byre-cock crows; he feels the light.
>
> So, in this water mixed with dust,
> The byre-cock spirit crows from trust
> That death will change because it must;
>
> . . . . . we have no home,
>
> Only a beauty, only a power,
> Sad in the fruit, bright in the flower,
> Endlessly erring for its hour,
>
> But gathering, as we stray, a sense
> Of Life, so lovely and intense,
> It lingers when we wander hence,
>
> That those who follow feel behind
> Their backs, when all before is blind,
> Our joy, a rampart to the mind.[27]

His life was whole, in the fullest sense, and deeply humane. His poetry, like his life, has certain lines that remain with one, and ring absolutely true. They fall on ear and mind as a sincere, honest thoughtful man's message; his attempt to give a lead in the dark. The last line of the poem above is of that kind.

His life now became increasingly secluded. In 1949 he had influenza leading to pneumonia, with appendicitis to follow. But he kept up his cheerful, informative and full-hearted correspondence with old friends and young.[28,29] In 1960 his wife Constance died at the age of 93. He missed her regulation of his life and a presence that was commanding. His daughter Judith ministered to him, while he gathered doctorates and other honours. In 1961 he was appointed a Companion of the Royal Society of Literature, and received the William Foyle prize for his *The Bluebells and Other Verse,* of the same year:

> A miracle unspeakable of flower
> That tears in the heart's anguish answered to.[30]

A prize came too from the National Book League in 1964.

He died on 12th May 1967 in his eighty-ninth year, and his ashes were placed in Poets' Corner at Westminster Abbey. This was not strictly in accordance with his wishes for he had written (very similarly to Swinburne):

> Let no religious rite be done or read
> In any place for me when I am dead,
> But burn my body into ash, and scatter
> The ash in secret into running water,
> Or on the windy down, and let none see;
> And then thank God that there's an end of me.

Yet he did feel that there is something in us that communicates (at least for a while) with those we love, after our death, and that something survives, be it but a few words in a book:

> To those beloved, his spirit's daily bread;
> Then that, too, fades; in book or deed a spark
> Lingers, then that, too, fades; then all is dark.[31]

But the best words with which to end are those of "An Epilogue" which sum him up:

> I have seen flowers come in stony places
> And kind things done by men with ugly faces,
> And the gold cup won by the worst horse at the races,
> So I trust, too.[32, 33]

Notes

1 If Housman, who Masefield admired (cf. chapter 17, above), had been a Gemini, perhaps he would have been a happier poet(!)

2 As was Housman's father.

3 On the grounds of expense, probably, since he had just about settled by then.

4 The present writer recalls using psalms in the same way when "square-bashing" in the RAF.

5 *John Masefield*; edited by D L Dodds. Arthurian Poets Series. Woodbridge, Boydell Press, 1994, cf. 3-5 (etc.); 196: "My Library: Volume One" (sonnet); 197 "Caer Ocvran" (sonnet): "The heart that beat to beauty is forgiven".

6 J C Powys. *The Secret of Self-Development*. Haldeman-Julius (USA), 1926; Village Press, 1974. Public libraries, too, play their part, here.

7 Described by Masefield in Chapter 17 above.

8 Crocker Wight. *John Masefield*: a bibliographical description of his first, limited, signed and special editions. Boston (USA), the Library of the Boston Athenaeum, 1992, 1-4 (etc.)

9 John Shirley Quirk sings them, accompanied by Viola Tunnard, on a Saga recording of 1963, the sleeve-note of which is acknowledged.

10 Of which Anne Jemima Clough, sister of Arthur Hugh Clough, was the first Principal.

11 Author of "The Playboy of the Western World", "Riders to the Sea", and "Deirdre of the Sorrows."

12 Always a sign of an ill-advised, if idealistic, early manhood.

13 See Chapter 17. above.

14 *John Masefield : Selected Poems*, with a preface by John Betjeman. Heinemann/Book Club Associates, 1978, 289-290; Heinemann have been his main English publishers.

15 "My Faith in Woman Suffrage", a speech delivered in the Queen's Hall, Feb. 14. 1910. Ref. 8, 21, Item 10.

16 Ref. 14, 157-9

17 Touched on in Chapter 17, above

18 Ref, 14, 205

19 The quotation is taken from Constance Babington Smith's biography, *John Masefield: a*

life, 1978.

20 As the American edition calls it. Ref. 8, 113, Item 65c.

21 See Ref. 5, 198-261

22 *The Midnight Folk*, Puffin edition, 13-17

23 See Chapter 17, above.

24 *The Coming of Christ*. Heinemann, 1928, 9 (Item 71b, Ref. 8, 124-5)

25 "How can I, that girl standing there/ My attention fix ...?" (Yeats: "Politics"), not to speak of Maud Gonne, Iseult Gonne, Lady Gregory, his wife, Dorothy Wellesley ...

26 Of TV fame more recently, and so familiar to today's children or young parents.

27 *Oxford Book of English Verse*, 2nd ed., 1939 (1948), 1113-5. It is illustrative of Masefield's riches that Ref. 14, above, can omit it.

28 "Courtly" always in manner, as Geoffrey Handley-Taylor puts it.

29 Cf. *Letters to Reyna*; edited William Buchan. Buchan & Enright, 1983 (cited above in Chapters 2 and 17)

30 Ref. 14, 300-1

31 Sonnet XXX, Ref. 14, 176

32 Based on lectures given at the National Portrait Gallery, 29th July 1993; Malvern Public Library, 29th May 1996, and the Burgage Hall, Ledbury, 1st June 1996. See also Appendix III.

33 In 1994 a plaque was dedicated at Preston Church to mark the place of his baptism. It is a fine relief profile of Masefield, provided by courtesy of the John Masefield Society and Blackwells of Oxford.

19. YEATS

W B Yeats, another Gemini, was born in Dublin on 13th June 1865. and died on the 28th January 1939, when the Second World War was looming, a little chagrined that he had not enjoyed the longevity of some of his ancestors. The year of his birth saw the death of Elizabeth Gaskell and the assassination of Lincoln. It saw the publication of Arnold's *Essays in Criticism*, Newman's *The Dream of Gerontius*, Swinburne's *Atalanta in Calydon*, Ruskin's *Sesame and Lilies*, Clough's *Letters and Remains*, volumes of Carlyle's opus on Frederick II, and Gifford Palgrave's *A Year's Journey through Central Eastern Arabia*. He was brought up in an Irish Protestant family, much of whose time was divided between London[1] and Ireland. His father was a painter, as was the poet's brother. The cultural influences were Pre-Raphaelite and, by remove, Romantic, to which were added Irish political and literary history and Celtic mythology, the latter background being deepened by his later friendship with Lady Gregory, given her close interest in the folklore of Ireland. Early portraits show the poet as a withdrawn, dreamy idealist, lost in reverie[2], an image that over the years would come to be overlaid by those of the dramatist, the man of affairs, the Senator, and Nobel Prize winner, the broadcaster, with proud scorn in stare and hair, (cf. his late photographs), and the poet of powerful, contemporary manner, of his last twenty years: the poet of colloquial immediacy, high disciplined rhetoric, terse concision as tutored by Pound[3,4] and almost majestical scorn - but still with the romantic idealism underlying it, the high ideals of the Muse, with which he had been informed in youth and was never to lose. But the evidence of those overlays illustrates how successfully he could "remake" himself.

His work falls into five, perhaps six categories.

1. He is the poet of the *Celtic Twilight*. influenced by the Pre-Raphaelites and Irish folk-lore; the ardent disciple of Blake, Shelley and Morris. In *Ideas of Good and Evil*, his essays of 1903, he writes of the symbolism of Shelley's poetry - of caves, and moons, and journeys down rivers in drifting vessels - and pictures Shelley lost in reverie in "some chapel, of the Star of infinite desire."[5] In another essay he describes Morris as "the Happiest of the Poets"[6], and in the same book he has pieces on the imagination and art of Blake, reminding us that in 1863 (with E J Ellis) he edited Blake, and that, as Masefield has recorded, he had examples of Blake's graphic work on his walls.[7] Thus there is a consistency, a learning, a continuing thread, that binds his work. It can be seen too that, as was said of Sir Francis Palgrave[8], "*he worked.*" It is worth noting that his father encouraged him to concentrate on such studies and his poetry, rather than to earn his living in mind-draining toil, as also, that the fact that he

did not marry until he was 52 assisted that single-minded pre-occupation with his Muse.[9]

Typical poems of this period are "Down by the Salley Gardens" of 1889, well-known in its musical setting; "When you are old", "A Dream of Death" and "The Lake Isle of Innisfree", collected in *The Rose* of 1893, "The Cap and Bells", which he says meant a great deal to him,[10] "He wishes for the Cloths of Heaven" and "The Song of Wandering Aengus" (1899):

I will find out where she has gone
...
And pluck till time and times are done
The silver apples of the moon,
The golden apples of the sun.

In one of several poems with Indian reference, "Anashuya and Vijaya", occurs a symbol characteristic of his work at this period:

And, ever pacing on the verge of things,
The phantom, Beauty, in a mist of tears

There are certain transitional poems, too, where he seems to be adapting his style, prior to the influence that Pound had on him. *In the Seven Woods* (1904) has "The Folly of Being Comforted" and "Never Give all the Heart" but also "Adam's Curse" where both the craft of the poet and the Muse are discussed in a much more concrete, immediate manner:

... A line will take us hours maybe;
Yet if it does not seem a moment's thought,
Our stitching and unstitching have been naught.
Better go down upon your marrow-bones
And scrub a kitchen pavement, or break stones
Like an old pauper, in all kinds of weather...

– to which the lady replies:

... To be born woman is to know -
Although they do not talk of it at school -
That we must labour to be beautiful.

At the same period he was writing -

2. The earlier of his *plays* – a major part of his *poetic* oeuvre – perforce briefly touched upon in Chapter 17, above, and –

3. The main part of his *narrative poetry*, most of which relates to his earlier pre-occupations, including as it does *The Wanderings of Oisin* (1889), a poem in three books, the first in rhyming octosyllabic couplets, with lyric passages; the second in rhyming pentameters:

...'And which of these
Is the Island of Content?' 'None knows', she said;
And on my bosom laid her weeping head.

– the third in long-lined quatrains of an immense fluency. There is an equally lyric flow about *Baile and Aillinn* (1903), and period "Celtic" glow about the 1906 version of *The Shadowy Waters*.[11] The succinct *The Two Kings*, which sees Edain opting for a love that is mortal, the more precious because of its brevity –

> What can they know of love that do not know
> She builds her nest upon a narrow ledge
> Above a windy precipice?

– is a transition between the Celtic/mythical material (and the dreamy manner associated with it) and *The Gift of Harun Al-Rashid* (1923), written in his later style, a few years after his marriage, embodying both his happiness and what he learnt from his wife:

> ... a woman who so shares
> Your thirst for those crabbed mysteries,
> So strains to look beyond our life ...
> And yet herself can seem youth's very fountain,
> Being all brimmed with life ...
> And thereupon his bounty gave what now
> Can shake more blossom from autumnal chill
> Than all my bursting springtime knew ...
> All, all, those gyres and cubes and midnight things
> Are but a new expression of her body
> Drunk with the bitter sweetness of her youth.

4. Phase 4 – the middle period for his poetry – sees his work charged with the fierceness of politics and public affairs as with the empathy and pride of friendship. It was his privilege to know many people involved in the cultural life of his country, whose names reverberate; that, arguably, was more possible in a country with Ireland's population than it would be in England (before the television and mass communication of today). It is true that he was well known in England and America as well, but it was Ireland that gave him the subjects and people he wrote about, whether or not he distanced himself from them. In his notes to the *Collected Poems* he speaks of the political, literary/religious and artistic controversies with which his work is involved; the frenzy over the production of Synge's *Playboy*, the Parnell controversy, and the dispute over the Hugh Lane pictures. "To a wealthy Man ..." concerns the pictures; "To a Shade", Parnell; "On those that hated the 'Playboy'" needs no exposition. "September 1913" gathers up his feelings in its refrain:

> Romantic Ireland's dead and gone,
> It's with O'Leary in the grave.

– an illustration of his sonorous rhetoric and ballad-like declamation. As for the impetus of friendship, it sees him at his best, whether in "Friends" or "A Memory of Youth":

Believing every word I said,
I praised her body and her mind
Till pride had made her eye grow bright,
And pleasure made her cheeks grow red...
Nothing but darkness overhead.[12]

In *The Wild Swans at Coole* (1919) it is friendship that is predominant. The beautiful title poem is followed by "In Memory of Major Robert Gregory" where not only his benefactor's son but other friends are reviewed with gravity and dignity. In Stanza III: "Lionel Johnson comes the first to mind", who he knew in London in the 1880s; in IV: "And that enquiring man John Synge comes next,/ That dying chose the living world for text"/; in V it is the turn of his uncle George Pollexfen; from XII it is Gregory who has to "Share in that discourtesy of death", Yeats' reverie on which climaxes in Stanza XI:

Some burn damp faggots, others may consume
The entire combustible world in one small room ...

"The Fisherman", a spare, lean poem, is in the same mood. In "His Phoenix", "Her Praise", "Broken Dreams" his reverie invokes past (and continuing) affection, while "The People" returns to public affairs, yet involves his "phoenix", too. In the same volume there is sign of a return to his earliest preoccupations. In "Ego Dominus Tuus" he muses on Keats; in "The Phases of the Moon" he mentions Pater and:

... the candle-light
From the far tower where Milton's Platonist
Sat late, or Shelley's visionary prince:
The lonely light that Samuel Palmer engraved.
An image of mysterious wisdom won by toil ...

It was as though in middle age (in 1919 he was 54) he was anxious to secrete the inheritance.

In his best work his feeling is always balanced not only by his technical skill[13] but by a sense of irony and balance, an instinct for restraint and proportion. Thus in *Michael Robartes and the Dancer* (1921), the title poem has a dozen lines of rhetoric by the male speaker followed by the woman's "You mean they argued." Thus he has the best of both worlds: the hook catches at us, and seems to give a mocking prick at the poet's assumptions, yet he is able to indulge the rhetoric and state the assumptions as well. In the same volume we find stately passion in "Easter 1916" and the delicate poignancy of "On a Political Prisoner" on Constance Markiewicz:

When long ago I saw her ride
Under Ben Bulben to the meet,
The beauty of her country-side
With all youth's lonely wildness stirred,
She seemed to have grown clean and sweet
Like any rock-bred, sea-borne bird ...

– with that masterly control of rhythm and conjunction of sounds so expertly worked out which we come to take for granted in his poems. "A Prayer for my Daughter"[14] is ceremonious, a thing like Mozart's 39th symphony.

> In courtesy I'd have her chiefly learned;
> Hearts are not had as gifts but hearts are earned
> ... many a poor man that has roved,
> Loved and thought himself beloved,
> From a glad kindness cannot take his eyes.

5. *The Tower* (1928) inaugurates his final period, that comes to have a panache, even devil-may-care, take-it-or-leave it attitude at times, as in "High Talk" or the second of three marching songs, "The soldier takes pride ..."; yet at its best it is as ceremonious as ever. What could be more ordered, in the best Romantic tradition than the ode-like structures of "Sailing from Byzantium", "Byzantium", "All Soul's Night", "Among School Children"? - and this even if one contests the ebullient claim: "We were the last romantics" which he writes in "Coole Park and Ballylee, 1931". There is the same emotional control in these odes as in so many of the poems of friendship and "politics" mentioned above. It emerges again in the poem beginning "The light of evening, Lissadell", where he reflects again on Constance Markiewicz and Eva Gore-Booth. What gnomic wisdom there is, likewise, in the shorter pieces such as "Swift's Epitaph", "For Anne Gregory", or "The Choice":

> The intellect of man is forced to choose
> Perfection of the life or of the work

The ore-rich lines of "What Then" and "An Acre of Grass" are equally of this character:

> Let the fool's rage, I swerved in naught,
> Something to perfection brought"
> ...... "What then?

or in the capacity he shows to reshape his art in his seventies, even while adhering to his earliest agenda, and thus enriching the inheritance:

> Grant me an old man's frenzy,
> Myself must I remake
> Till I am Timon and Lear
> Or that William Blake
> Who beat upon the wall
> Till Truth obeyed his call ...[15]

In "Under Ben Bulben" familiar names appear for one last time:

> Calvert and Wilson, Blake and Claude,
> Prepared a rest for the people of God,
> Palmer's phrase, but after that
> Confusion fell upon our thought.

Yeats will have known that, for a year or two in the Shoreham Valley, the "valley of vision", c1825-35, Samuel Palmer, friend and disciple of Blake, had realised with Calvert and Richmond something of an earthly paradise, with which Morris, too, would have empathised. Equally Blakean in background, in recalling "The Sick Rose", are the chambermaid's two songs in the very unusual and intriguing sequence based on "The Three Bushes". The "Crazy Jane" poems, with their ballad-like rhythms and directness, their strident physicality, and telling use of refrain, deal with related impulses, whilst extending yet further his artistic range. We close with two poems which show the elder poet refining to the end his Romantic affections and ideals (of both the large and the small "R" variety) with consummate mastery and dignity, equal to the language of a Prospero.

> No dark tomb-haunter once; her form all full
> As though with magnanimity of light,
> Yet a most gentle woman ...

he says of a sculpture of Maud Gonne in "A Bronze Head", or with a finality of simplicity, as he bolts and bars the shutters and looks at the familiar books on his shelves:

> ... everything outside us is
> *Mad as the mist and snow*[16]

6. The resume of his poems and plays, indicative as it is of his immense gifts and range, and the extent of his oeuvre, yet omits his prose works: the stories, the essays, the *Autobiographies* (collected, 1955) in which he writes so eloquently of Synge, Lionel Johnson, Dowson, George Moore, Wilde and Lady Gregory, Florence Farr and Maud Gonne, or *A Vision*, his remarkable excursion into occult philosophy, published in 1925, on the symbolism of which so much of his subsequent work is based.[17] In all these genres he remains the poet, while as poet *per se* he bids to be the most important writing in English since the High Romantics, with the possible exceptions of Browning and Tennyson, placing Swinburne and Hopkins only just below the three of them. His range is wide; he speaks to many different kinds of reader, both read aloud and on the page, and his high (and Romantic) view of his vocation (not to speak of his immense fervour) makes him enduringly inspiring.[18]

Notes

1 In Woodstock and Blenheim roads, Bedford Park (close to the present author's birthplace and school) before his sojourn at Woburn Buildings, cf. chapters 17 & 18 above.

2 Cf. the drawing of J B Yeats, c1894 (cf. W B Yeats: *Autobiographies*, Macmillan, 1955, facing page 336)

3 Ezra Pound met him 1908; acted as his secretary 1913, and Yeats stayed with him in 1915 and 1916 at Stone Cottage. (cf. A N Jeffares: *W B Yeats: a new biography*. Arena, 1990, 159 (etc.)

4 Later they met at Rapallo in 1928, cf. Hone, J: *W B Yeats 1865-1939*. Macmillan, 1942, 394

5 W B Yeats: *Ideas of Good and Evil*. A H Bullen, 1903, 90-141 (140)

6 op.cit., 70-89 (The assumption in the title is intriguing, yet if anyone *deserved* to be happy it was Morris, for his generous, industrious application of his gifts to interests not solely his own.)

7 op.cit., 168-225 and cf. Chapters 17 and 18 above.

8 See Chapter 8

9 Not only did it keep the R(r)omantic flame in trim; it avoided the impingement of the more day to day aspects of domesticity upon bardic felicity.

10 Notes to the *Collected Poems*. 2nd edition. Macmillan, 1950 (1950)

11   For the 1911 version see the *Collected Plays*. Macmillan, 2nd edition 1952 (1953)

12 These several poems are in *Responsibilities*, 1914

13 There are many testimonies to the way he worked over his poems, often from prose drafts, often speaking the lines aloud, and writing out many versions (much like Dylan Thomas after him and, a little, like Hopkins before him).

14 Donald Davie thought he was at his best in such mid-career work.

15 "An Acre of Grass."

16 "Mad as the Mist and Snow"; the italics in the refrain are Yeats' own.

17 A brave attempt to construct a symbolic system of historical and astrological bricks, arguably both a hotch-potch and, at its best, as creatively, "poetically" stimulating as the I CHING.

18 Subject of the Richmond Reading of 1st November 1990 and based on lectures at the Richmond upon Thames College rather than on Pearce, B.L. "Yeats: a man who lost the way." *The Voice of Youth, 2* (6) Summer 1954, 11-14, an essay in youthful arrogance.

APPENDIX I

THE GOLDEN TREASURY

In the Summer of 1860, on a walking holiday with Tennyson, Francis Turner Palgrave conceived the idea of his anthology of the "best songs and lyrical poems in the English language" and of presenting them in compact, portable form, not as library-only tomes bound in calf. Reasons of space, as much as the sub-title's explication of emphasis, will have dictated the exclusion of narrative, epic and dramatic work, as well as the humorous, satiric or specifically religious categories, the last of which he was to treat later in his Treasury of Sacred Song. It is the poetry of feeling matched with form, and of the lyric that treats of a single emotion or idea, that he sought for through an immense range of material, including both existing anthologies and the collections of individual poets. The concept of "lyrical" he held to imply song-likeness, besides a poem turning on some single thought, feeling or situation, and looked for excellence "rather in the whole than in the parts". He divided the book into four sections:

I   early 1500s to about 1616 (the Book of Shakespeare)

II   1616 to 1700 (the Book of Milton)

III 18th century (the Book of Gray)

IV c1800-1850 (the Book of Wordsworth)

It is a practical scheme but, if one *has* to select representative figures in this fashion we might nowadays elect not Gray but Pope.

Passionate man as his early work shows he could be[1], a man (with doubts) of faith and a hymnwriter, he steers a selective path between matter "too warm" and too obsessively religious, as he saw it. For better or worse, therefore, we see that the anthology accords with the public image of a man of taste and position: son of Sir Francis, the noted historian: student of Balliol, Fellow of Exeter; assistant to Gladstone; who earned his keep in the Education Department, Whitehall, and lived at York Gate, Regent's Park. Creatively that taste and position worked to his disadvantage, but *of* his taste, and judgment, and its successful application to his anthology, there can be little doubt. It is attested by the way he sifted through so much work and selected what most critics have conceded *was* the best, and found the occasional poem of less known writers, as well as the best of what was better known, subject to the restrictions of the above criteria. He did omit Donne and Blake, it is true, but added them (and

Christopher Smart) in a later edition. It is attested by the Treasury's continuing in print since its publication and in schoolroom use for a hundred years[2]. It is attested by writers as diverse as Graham Greene or Richard Church having had a copy in their pocket as they set off on an African journey or rested their back against an English haystack. Jowett and Frederick Temple praised it. Alice Meynell "began" with it. The original (1861) work stops at 1850, and specifically excludes his contemporaries, as well as pre-16th century work, a stricture involving the loss of Anglo-Saxon poems such as "Wulf" and "Deor" as well as Chaucer and Dunbar. *The Second Series,* published in 1897, the year of his death, covers his contemporaries, but has never received the critical imprimatur accorded the original work. It is the work of an aged man; he is more limited as to period, and it is notoriously difficult to judge of one's peers. It includes many whose contributions would not have been missed[3]; and omits Henley, Yeats, Kipling, Alice Meynell, and Francis Thompson. The omission of Hopkins is, of course, due to Bridges not releasing his friend's work till 1918. He made every attempt to include Swinburne, whom he admired. It is to his credit that he includes Clough[4]; Clare, including his moving "I am ....", and a generous selection from Christina Rossetti and both Brownings. Robert, like Clough, a friend, was sometimes too didactic and obscure, or morally generous, for Palgrave's taste. He includes "Two in the Campagna" though not "Fra Lippo Lippi" or "The Statue and the Bust"[5]. In these, as in many cases, he might argue that it was length, not taste necessarily that compelled their exclusion. Patmore he gives more space than most would now allow him, but cf. the Patmore essay. Fashion can be arbitrary and the reader may like to glance at "Winter" or "A Farewell" before settling for the received opinion. At all times, indeed, FTP is concerned with *poems*, not an author's life, background, or reputation, and this is one of his great strengths. He and his band of collaborators, Woolner, George Miller and Tennyson, *read each poem aloud* in making their selection, and indeed it is only by so doing, in our age or his, that any poem can be brought to judgment. The proof of the method is in the *Treasury* (first series) which served our literature for four to five generations. Its influence was great, *and* good, provided we acknowledge that it, arguably, focused too much attention on the song or lyric as the acme of the Muse and the anthologisable item. It might be felt to have influenced the Georgians and their associates adversely, if it had encouraged them to repress experiment and rugged individualism, and to eschew the longer poem, but amongst them there were many who wrote dramatic and narrative verse, and who sought for a social realism alien to the *Treasury* which they carried in their rucksacks.

Palgrave sought to educate, evaluate, and to extend awareness. His success in setting standards and in bringing poetry a wider audience has been beneficial to writers and readers alike. Only an élitist might wish that the Muse's cultivation could have been kept as a secret "craft" which only initiates had the right to ply, after a long apprenticeship, though indeed in our own day a return to some such concept might not be such a bad thing[6].

The pros and cons of the *Treasury*'s influence are perhaps best seen in comparison with one or two other anthologies. Palgrave's emphasis on the poem as sole criterion - and the way his separation of an author's pieces forces us to a similar evaluation[7] - can be contrasted with the authorial and chronological arrangements of 'Q's *Oxford Book of English Verse*, Larkin's *Oxford Book of Twentieth Century English Verse* and Grant Duff's *Victorian Anthology* of 1902. 'Q's book, given to the writer as a grammar school prize in 1949, has had considerable influence on earlier and (with its 1939 2nd edition) later twentieth-century generations, and would be his own chosen companion. But it could draw on Palgrave and by 1939 feature later work; look down a longer telescope. Its space is so much greater: 1199 pages to Palgrave's 381 (in 1894); it does not pine for African travel or crave to slide into the pocket on rambles - nor do the other two titles. What moving tribute 'Q' pays to his predecessor's achievement:

> Few of my contemporaries can erase - or would wish to erase – the dye their minds took from the late Mr Palgrave's *Golden Treasury*: and he who has returned to it again and again with an affection born of companionship on many journeys must remember not only what the Golden Treasury includes, but the moment when this or that poem appealed to him, and even how it lies on the page.[8]

For that alone, if the Treasury warmed and informed a subsequent anthologist of such substance, we can be thankful and credit it as positive influence.

Larkin's book differs from Palgrave and 'Q' in its hospitality to work that illustrates its period in social and political terms, not purely in gem-like artefacts. Could we claim intrinsic poetic merit, for example, for the pieces by G.D.H. Cole, Alex Comfort or Edward Shanks, pertinent but scarcely meeting Palgrave's generation-transcending criteria? It is true that the period, and hence the poetry, in question, has its own distinct character. Yet a concern with narrative or anecdotal elements, as opposed to purely intrinsic technical merits, is also a feature of Grant Duff's *Victorian Anthology* with its invitation to serendipity. It is based on authors and well structured, though it does include far more duffers (to a late 20th century judgment anyhow) than is the case even in Palgrave's second (or 1897) selection. It is what we might expect of a Victorian anthologist, and does not this illustrate the extent to which Palgrave transcends his age by his own severely objective and even austere criteria. If that has been his influence (and I write as one whose interest extends to authors as much as to artefacts) it cannot but have been good.[9]

Notes

1 Cf. his prose masterpiece *The Passionate Pilgrim* (1858:1926); or the pieces from *Idyls and Songs*, eg. in *Palgrave: Selected Poems*; edited with an introduction by B L Pearce. Brentham Press, 1985.

2 W. Bell, J.H. Fowler, E.A.G. Lamborn and C.B. Wheeler were amongst those who published commentaries on the *Treasury* (c1904-1935) already well served as it was with Palgrave's own judicious notes.

3 Philip Larkin records how A.E. Housman marked his copy on these lines, indicating how thoroughly he had read this *Second Series*. Larkin, P. *Required Writing: miscellaneous pieces 1955 - 1982*. Faber, 1983, 198-203

4 In Palgrave's edition of Clough (1862) he included pieces a little too "warm" for his widow Blanche's liking.

5 Cf. Pearce, B.L. *Browning and F.T. Palgrave some notes*. In Browning Society Notes, 21, 1991 - 1992, 65-69

6 Cf. eg. Russell, P. *The Lovelessness of Recent Poetry, Ore* (50), Autumn 1995, 25-32

7. His juxtaposition of pieces has often been praised though it can be confusing not to find an author's work all in one place.

8 From the Preface by 'Q' (Sir Arthur Quiller-Couch) to the 1st edition of October 1900 of the *OBEV*, reprinted in the edition of 1939.

9 Based on the author's paper Glow and Afterglow, "the criteria and influence of the Golden Treasury" in *Acumen* (24) January 1996, 23-26

APPENDIX II

JUBILEE VERSES : SOME POEMS
WRITTEN FOR THE 1887 JUBILEE

The difficulty in raising the head of steam necessary to achieve anything of real poetic merit is always a problem where "set" topics are concerned, even for writers of distinction, Apart from the constraints imposed by a given subject, there is the need for clarity of expression and regularity of structure if public accessibility is to be assumed. The key question in regard to tribute verse is this: Is it an adequate example of the writer's own style?

But another kind of interest attaches to such pieces: that of the topics, persons, and places to which they refer. In the Golden Jubilee poems, certain themes emerge clearly. Victoria, as we would expect, is a symbol for the events (actual and as mythically-conceived) of her reign. The concern is with the achievements of nation and empire, and the references have a wide range. There is the preoccupation with science, commerce and manufacture, and a fascination with invention and industrial progress; with prosperity, too, intermingled with philanthropy. There is a name-dropping which, superficial as it can be, betokens a strong emotional response to the associations of place. Asia, especially India, seems to have haunted the British mind. Though successes are dwelt on, we find the same preoccupation with defeats (Khyber, the early stages of the Mutiny, Khartoum, in this case) which recurs throughout our literature from the Battle of Maldon. Thus there is much to interest the patriot and the historian as well as the reader of poetry.

Tennyson, the Poet Laureate, duly paid his tribute, though it was to be expected that in his late seventies he might not maintain the standard of his *Ode to the Queen* (1851) or magnificent *Ode on the Death of the Duke of Wellington* (1852). Tennyson mentions a hospital; exhorts to philanthropy, cites previous reigns of similar length; has visions of an: "Imperial Institute,/Rich in symbol, in ornament,/Which may speak to the centuries"; refers to Commerce, Science and Empire, with capital initials; mentions manufactures and the colonies. Two of the best lines occur in the final stanza, added at the Queen's request. Much else, though worthy in sentiment (and set by Stanford) is of indifferent merit.

F.T. Palgrave, who was Professor of Poetry at Oxford at the time of the Jubilee, and who had sought Tennyson's advice when compiling his *Golden Treasury*, had in his ambitious *Ode for the Twenty-First of June 1887* passages of greater poetic appeal:

The Girl from care in youth's sweet sleep withdrawn
Wakes to a crown at dawn!

He, too, refers to Commerce and Science; also calling up the electric telegraph, railways and steamships, electric light ("Lo Commerce with the golden girdling chain/That links all nations for the good of each;/While Science boasts her silent lightning speech"), Alma, the Khyber, and the death of Gordon, the mention of whom gives some indication of the strong feeling in the country at his betrayal. The reference to "palm and pine" anticipates Kipling's in *Recessional*.[1]

It was inevitable that William McGonagall would wish to pay his tribute in that manner which is so his own: "And as this is her first Jubilee Year,/And will be her last, I rather fear;/Therefore, sound drums and trumpets cheerfully,/Until the echoes are heard o'er land and sea." He mentions "dominions" and lauds Victoria as the "Empress of India" but otherwise it is all "shout and cheer".

In contrast to the more personal, often elusive context of poetry today, people like Tennyson, and McGonagall in his way, were public figures, expected to make some statement on events. A younger man, like A.E. Housman, with less sense of a ceremonial task to perform, could thus be better placed. In his "1887" we do have an adequate example of a writer's own style. As a specimen of his down-to-earth manner (so deliberately cultivated), his vigorous rhymes and thumping rhythms, it fits perfectly naturally into the *Shropshire Lad* sequence, published in 1896:

> Oh, God will save her, fear you not:
> Be you the men you've been,
> Get you the men your fathers got,
> And God will save the Queen.

Besides the hilltop beacons, Housman mentions Asia, the Nile, and the "Lads of the Fifty-Third".

Amongst other tributes to the occasion - not least that on the souvenir medal struck by W.J. Taylor, of Birmingham, and drawn to our attention by Mark Jones - "A Lothian Justice's *Jubilee and other Rhymings*" are of particular interest, anticipating the Channel Tunnel, albeit with some alarm, and hoping to see Ireland and Britain in closer accord.[2] The Australian Henry Halloran's *Jubilee Ode* has perhaps equal merit to Palgrave's, with not dissimilar references.[3] Many of these themes recur in 1897 - Francis Thompson's fine *Ode* is crammed with them.[4]

Notes
1 See also Chesterton's *Post-Recessional*
2 Pearce, B.L. (ed.), *Hail to the Queen*. Magwood, 1987, [R.A. MacFie] 18-19, 21.
3 Ref. 2, 15-17
4 Originally published in the *Journal* of the Royal Society of Arts, *CXXV* (5372) July 1987, 573-4

APPENDIX III

MASEFIELD'S TECHNIQUE

The Bunyan-esque conversion of Saul Kane in "The Everlasting Mercy" is conveyed with zest and great narrative and verbal accomplishment, even if it does contain passages that could have been omitted to advantage. No doubt he will have known of the Independent congregation at the Burgage hall, Ledbury, as well as others in England or America. There is a tremendous exuberance conveyed by the *repetitions* of:

> O Christ who holds the open gate
> O Christ who drives the furrow straight,
> O Christ the plough, O Christ the laughter...
> The everlasting mercy, Christ

– and a lovely image of the lily at the close.

He uses *proper names* for evocative appeal, directness, clarity, sometimes as Housman might; at others, for immediacy. Note the *alliteration* in the "Arthurian" sonnet "Caer Ocvran's second line:

> A heave of hill, once castled for a king

In "Sea Fever"s second verse note the *end rhyme, internal rhyme*, "call/all", "day/spray", *alliteration*, "clear call", "windy/white". the bubbling *"l" sounds* of "call" (thrice), "wild/all/clouds/flying/flung/blown/gulls", and the overall explosion of *sound-energy*, culminating in "the flung spray and the blown spume", using words of one or two syllables only.

"Port of Many Ships" is so full of rhythm that it is rather like a WS Gilbert patter song; its brilliance must have invited yet challenged Keel to set it to music so convincingly.

In "CLM" do the *"m" sounds* so evident in the first verse arise from a child's earliest attempts to murmur a sound representing its mother, and from half-conscious memories of maternal enfolding? Be that as it may note the splendid juxaposition of womb/my/mother's/made/me/man/months/human/common/some – and the unaccented sounds such as the "m"s in "womb" or "some" may be as telling as those of a more thrusting character. By the end of the poem, the last line – "O grave, keep shut lest I be shamed" needs only the one "m" in shamed to confirm the dominant murmuring consonant. The *assonance* of "grave" and "shamed" and *alliteration* of "shut" and "shamed" reaching resolution in the last syllable parallels Hopkins' cynghanned effect in "Fall, gall themselves, and gash gold-vermilion" in "The Windhover", and is a tribute to Masefield's powers.

In "The Passing Strange" he embodies in its three-lined stanzas – each with a common end rhyme – a gradual shift from vital life to stillness and term and then a shift back to concepts of life and joy again. It starts and ends with *alliteration*, for vowels can be as alliterative as consonants. The "lead in the dark" he gives us in the closing stanza – "our joy a rampart to the mind" – is reinforced by the alliteration of the two penultimate lines and by the "m" sounds in "rampart" and "mind" – which is to comment on the technique but not to explain the humanity and life-force behind it.

ACKNOWLEDGEMENTS

The author is appreciative of the help and kindness he has received from a great many people in connection with this book and the lectures on which it is based. They include:

John Cooper, Chief Education Officer, National Portrait Gallery, Dr D G C Allan of the RSA, Dr James Hogg of Salzburg University, William and Patricia Oxley, Rupert Loydell, Margaret and Ann Pearce, D Woolf and the Trustees of Coleridge's Cottage; Keats House, Hampstead, and the John Clare Society; Gemma Hunter, late Curator of the Orleans Gallery, Twickenham; Derek Jones, Jane Baxter, and the London Borough of Richmond upon Thames Libraries; Elaine Baly (Vivienne Browning), Roy Bolton, Mairi Calcraft-Rennie, Toba Mann, Michael Meredith, and other fellow members of the Browning Society; Alan Gaunt, Clyde Binfield, Daniel Jenkins and the late Donald Davie; Pamela McWilliam, Norman Longmate, Patricia Nicholls and Christine Pryer, Derek and Estelle Smith, Nia Taylor, Louise Rogers, John Skidmore, Sarah Curtis, Imogen McEvedy, A J Stirling, Glyn Pursglove, Elizabeth and Michael Foster, Roland Pilcher, Dennis Sargent, Hilary Caminer, Helen Nelson, Raymond and Elsbeth Shaw, Jane Stauch and the library of the Richmond upon Thames College, Peter Scupham and A C Bryer; Derek Palgrave and other fellow members of the Palgrave Society, Dr Megan Nelson (Canada), Mrs Geoffrey Barker, The British Library, Dorset County Library, Reading University Library; Margaret Tims and May Badman; Virginia Murray (archivist) and John Murray (publisher), the Master and Fellows of Trinity College, Cambridge; Susan Bennett (RSA Library), the Lincolnshire County Libraries; the Hopkins Society, Sean Street; the library of St Mary's University College, Strawberry Hill; Vivian Meynell and Benedict Meynell, respectively; John Heath-Stubbs and Eric Ratcliffe; David Urquhart and Mrs B Johnson; Keith Barber and Carolyn Huckfield; Peter Carter, Brian Nixon, Roma Woodnutt, W H Masefield and family; Audrey Napier-Smith; Geoffrey Handley-Taylor and Crocker Wight (both of them Masefield bibliographers) to whom the author is especially indebted; the library of the Boston (USA) Athenaeum, and fellow members of the John Masefield Society, in addition to those above; David Burgess, David and Margaret Hanley, Claire Tomalin and Christopher Fry; Mary and Lynn Willcocks; Bookfinders of Hastings and Bromley; R Knight, A C B Urwin, Dr T H R Cashmore, M Harper, G Baker, D H Simpson and other fellow members of the Borough of Twickenham Local History Society. Grateful acknowledgement is made to the Society of Authors, representatives of the literary estates of John Masefield and A E Housman, respectively, for permission to quote from copyright material.

INDEX

the references are to *chapters*